Prophet's Life
Prophetic fACTS, Prophetic Acts

Kollin L. Taylor

Social Aloe Ministries
Setting the captives free

Cover Design: Les (GermanCreative) of FIVERR

Copyright © 2024 Kollin L. Taylor
All rights reserved.
ISBN: 9798878488686

DEDICATION

To Mrs. Laurel E. Mc-Kenzie-Blidgen:

On July 4, 2019, without uttering a word, the Lord used you to communicate a message to me that showed that your final years were of tremendous prophetic significance. Those years were a grand prophetic act that pointed to Jesus's Words in Matthew 7:21-23. Therefore, even after your passing, the Lord Jesus still used you as an evangelist to reach the lost. Your legacy lives on...

Bible quotes are primarily from the King James Version (KJV) and secondarily from the English Standard Version (ESV). "Scripture quotations from the ESV® Bible (The Holy Bible, English Standard Version®), copyright © 2001 by Crossway, a publishing ministry of Good News Publishers. Used by permission.
All rights reserved.

The Prophet's Life

CONTENTS

	Acknowledgments	vii
	Prologue	ix
1	Father Abraham	Pg. 1
2	Moses	Pg. 5
3	Ezekiel	Pg. 23
4	Jeremiah	Pg. 43
5	Jesus	Pg. 54
	Epilogue	Pg. 66

ACKNOWLEDGMENTS

Heavenly Father, You gave me a dream on August 12, 2017. It was set in Jamaica, after my paternal grandmother's funeral. I was with one of my sisters, who lives in another country, and I had not seen her in the natural realm in about a decade. Another significant thing about the dream was me writing at a fervent pace. True to Your revelations, my grandmother passed away on December 29, 2021. Then I saw the sister You showed me in the dream, in Jamaica during the summer of 2022. That was also when You directed me to revise the manuscript for an upcoming book that I have been working on since 2018. I remember skipping the opportunity to go with my family to drag races at Vernam Field/Vernamfield in Clarendon, Jamaica. Instead, I stayed at home and spent the entire day writing fervently. At the time, those events seemed like the fulfillment of that special dream. Yet, in many ways, spending the day writing fervently was a prophetic act of what was to come.

Since around 2018, I have averaged about two published books per year. But thanks to this current assignment, You have had me write seven books in the last twelve months, which certainly fulfills the fervent pace threshold of the dream. I was not expecting to write another book for at least a few months, and certainly not this one. But I obeyed Your Holy Spirit's prompting to write this book while the ink was basically still wet on the pages of **FOUR Shades of Prophets: The Slippery Slope to Hell**, *and its predecessor by a month,* **Roles & Responsibilities for Today's Prophets (of the Lord)**. I had no time to celebrate their release as I had to get back to work, and You know why. So, I wholeheartedly thank You for this opportunity to glorify Your Son, my Lord and Savior, Jesus, the Christ.

The fulfillment of that dream reiterates that You are a

The Prophet's Life

Man of Your Word, for which I thank You and praise Your holy name. In some respects, the recent events gave me a taste of how Joseph may have felt when You moved on his behalf to begin fulfilling the dreams You had given him. As a result, in one day, You elevated Joseph from being a prisoner to Egypt's governor and the nation's second in command. That was a testament of what You would one day do for Jesus, Who is now seated at Your right hand in glory.

PROLOGUE

I find it laughable when people mention exercising their free will to make choices whenever God presents something to them. I am not sure what they are referring to. At least for me, free will is the ability to choose which God/god a person will serve. But once that decision is made, and the person is in service to that God/god, free will to that God/god is not as free as many people make it seem. Certainly, there are times when God gives people a choice, but why would a person who loves Jesus not want to do things per His will?

In Genesis 24, Abraham told his servant to find a wife for his son Isaac. When the servant asked what if the woman was not willing to return with him, Abraham said the servant would be released from his oath. The woman would be free to choose, but the Lord would also send an angel ahead of the servant to help with his success. The young woman was Rebekah, and despite the limited available information about the man the Lord wanted her to marry, she returned with Abraham's servant and married Isaac on the day they met. Their story foreshadowed how divine intervention, via angelic assistance, would play a role in another relationship. When Joseph found out that his betrothed was pregnant, the angel of the Lord assured him that it was okay to marry Mary because the Child she was carrying was of the Holy Spirit. When Joseph woke up from that dream, he did as the Lord commanded (Matthew 1:18-25). In both cases, God gave them a choice, but they chose to obey Him by coming into agreement with His will.

I was serving as a Battalion Coordinating Staff Officer as a First Lieutenant when the Executive Officer, "Major Luke," asked me to do something. He had the authority to command me to do the task, but he chose to ask instead. Despite his nuanced approach, I knew it was

The Prophet's Life

best to say yes. In fact, because of his approach, I was more motivated to go above and beyond to get the task done. That is how CHRISTians should react IF the Lord gives them a choice to do His will or their own.

Many people recite "The Lord's Prayer," as if, like Jesus in the Garden of Gethsemane, they promise to lay down their will for God's will to be done. Yet, when given opportunities to serve and glorify God, they speak about their free will as if they know better than God. Sometimes I refer to Jesus as the Lord Jesus Christ. That is to show that His name is Jesus, the anointed and only begotten Son of God. He is also Lord because I am His bondservant. So, in addition to being my Savior, Jesus is my Master. Sadly, many people refer to Jesus as their Lord, but they do not view and treat Him as such. That is why they speak about their free will. It is no wonder that Jesus said:

> *And why call ye Me, Lord, Lord, and do not the things which I say?* ~ Luke 6:46

There are consequences for opposing the Lord's will. That does not mean He afflicts those who do as they please. Sometimes it is simply a consequence of their actions, the same way the father let his son go and he ended up as a prodigal in the pigsty (Luke 15:11-32). Just imagine what happened to everyone who was offended with Jesus's teaching, so they walked away from Him and never followed Him again (John 6:66). The Lord respected their free will and let them go. Jesus immediately gave His apostles the opportunity to also walk away from Him. But they chose to stay when Simon Peter wisely responded, and the other apostles agreed:

> *Lord, to whom shall we go?*
> *Thou hast the Words of eternal life.*
> *And we believe and are sure that Thou art that Christ, the Son of the living God.* ~ John 6:68-69

The Prophet's Life

Despite the tone thus far, this book is not a chastisement of Believers for their abuse of free will in their relationship with the Lord Jesus. It is instead the foundation for the examination of the lives of prophets in the Bible, men and women who set aside their will for God's desires. To the disappointment of some people, it will not be an examination of what the prophets did in their daily lives when they were not prophesying. Instead, as the subtitle suggests, **Prophetic fACTS, Prophetic Acts** is about the deeply symbolic meanings behind some of the things the prophets did during their service to the Lord. Some things were clearly not of their desire or design but in pure obedience to the Lord their God. For prophets such as Moses and Jonah, their attempts to exercise their free will exposed them to grave consequences.

As we embark on this journey, I cannot think of a single person who the Lord asked if he or she wanted to serve Him as a prophet. For those whom the Bible tells how the Lord called them as prophets, please note that He called, they answered, and they NEVER looked back. And just in case you believe Isaiah volunteered to serve the Lord as a prophet, he was already a prophet when this unfolded:

> *Also I heard the voice of the Lord, saying, Whom shall I send, and who will go for Us?*
> *Then said I, Here am I; send me.* ~ Isaiah 6:8

CHAPTER 1
Father Abraham

By faith Abraham, when he was called to go out into a place which he should after receive for an inheritance, obeyed; and he went out, not knowing whither he went.
~ Hebrews 11:8

Abraham is the first person in the Bible whom God described as a prophet (Genesis 20:7). Interestingly, when that descriptor was first used, the Lord said it to King Abimelech of Gerar to describe Abraham. There is no mention of the Lord telling Abraham that He had called him as a prophet. But for Abraham, instead of him delivering prophecies, his life and prophetic ministry were filled with prophetic acts. Many of those acts pointed to Jesus, so even Abraham adhered to what was written eons later about prophecy:

...Worship God: for the testimony of Jesus is the Spirit of Prophecy. ~ Revelation 19:10

The Prophet's Life

When introduced to Abraham and his prophetic life, his name was Abram, and this was the Lord's command to him:

Get thee out of thy country, and from thy kindred, and from thy father's house, unto a land that I will shew thee: And I will make of thee a great nation, and I will bless thee, and make thy name great; and thou shalt be a blessing: And I will bless them that bless thee, and curse him that curseth thee: and in thee shall all families of the earth be blessed. ~ Genesis 12:1-3

That speaks of how Jesus would leave His Father in heaven to come down to earth. Abraham is referred to as a "Father of Nations," and as Isaiah prophesied, Jesus is the "Everlasting Father" (Isaiah 9:6). And through the Lord Jesus, we are blessed and become children of God (Galatians 3:26-29).

There were two instances where different men wanted Abraham's bride Sarai/Sarah. The first one was the pharaoh of Egypt followed by King Abimelech of Gerar (Genesis 12, 20). But the Lord would not allow those men to keep her. In fact, there were consequences for taking the Lord's prophet's wife. Likewise for the church, who is referred to as the Bride of Christ. Jesus will return for her without spot or wrinkle, and He will not allow the devil to have her (Ephesians 5:22-33). In fact, a major triggering event for Jesus's return is when His bride makes herself ready for Him (Revelation 19:6-8).

Abraham was also a warrior. He led his army of 318 men to fight to recover Lot and his family after their capture (Genesis 14). Similarly, Jesus came to set the captives free. And when He returns, it will be to judge, and as the Lord of Hosts, to wage war with His army against the forces of darkness (Isaiah 61:1-3, Revelation 19:11-21).

In addition, God cut a covenant with Abraham, which was symbolized by the circumcision of the foreskin

The Prophet's Life

(Genesis 17). It foreshadowed how we could have a Covenant with God, through the Lord Jesus Christ, one where the mark would be a circumcision of the heart (Romans 2:25-29, Hebrews 8-9, 12:24).

In Genesis 18 (16-33), when the Lord revealed His plans to Abraham to bring judgment upon Sodom and Gomorrah, the prophet interceded for the wicked people of Sodom. Abraham continually interceded until the Lord agreed to spare the city if He could find ten righteous people in it. After Jesus's death, burial, resurrection, and ascension into heaven, He is now seated at the right hand of the Heavenly Father making intercession for us (Romans 8:34). Now is a suitable time for a "praise break" if you have ever sinned, and instead of the death that you deserved, thanks to Jesus's intercession, you were given a chance to repent.

"PRAISE BREAK!!!"

Even though it was not the end of His life, this chapter ends with one of Abraham's most significant prophetic acts. It symbolized a decision the Heavenly Father would have to make about Jesus, His only begotten Son. Abraham endured an arduous twenty-four-year wait, and went through many trials, before the Lord blessed him with the promised son, Isaac. But just when it seemed as if Abraham could relax during the advanced years of his life, this happened:

> *And it came to pass after these things, that God did tempt Abraham, and said unto him, Abraham: and he said, Behold, here I am.*
> *And He said, Take now thy son, thine only son Isaac, whom thou lovest, and get thee into the land of Moriah; and offer him there for a burnt offering upon one of the mountains which I will tell thee of.* ~ Genesis 22:1-2

The Prophet's Life

Abraham willing obeyed God's command by making the painful decision to sacrifice his beloved son. That was until the Lord stopped him and provided a ram for Abraham to sacrifice instead. Sin's wage is death. And just like how God spared Isaac by providing a ram in lieu of him was how Yahweh offered His Son, Jesus, the Lamb of God, to take our place and die, so that like Isaac, we may live instead. For those who still cannot fathom that concept, here is a more palatable and understandable contemporary example. It is like a bodyguard who makes the conscious decision beforehand that he or she is willing to die in place of the person he or she is sworn to protect.

Jesus came to the earth with the willingness to give His life so others may live. Some men get married with the mindset that they will give their lives for their wives, which also points back to Jesus, about Whom it is written:

Husbands, love your wives, even as Christ also loved the church, and gave Himself for it. ~ Ephesians 5:25

Abraham, and even his son Isaac, were both involved in prophetic acts for God's glory. For Abraham, as a prophet, instead of a life and ministry filled with him prophesying on the Lord's behalf through spoken words, most of his prophecies were through prophetic acts. But as you will see, even among the prophets who prophesied verbally and in written formats, their lives were also filled with prophetic fACTS and prophetic acts.

Chapter 2
Moses

And the Lord said unto Moses,
See, I have made thee a god to Pharaoh:
and Aaron thy brother shall be thy prophet.
~ Exodus 7:1

The Lord God called Moses in a way that is illustrative of a prophet's limited free will. Moses was a reluctant prophet who tried various things to escape from God's calling, to include him saying:

Oh, my Lord, please send someone else. ~ Exodus 4:13 (ESV)

The Lord could have respected Moses's free will and simply moved on to someone else. But at what costs? For one thing, Moses's mighty ministry, to include the esteem he holds in Israel's and the world's history, would have been passed on to someone else. But again, at what costs? Has someone ever enjoyed a measure of success that you know you could have had IF you had simply obeyed God? How did it make you feel to see someone else

The Prophet's Life

capitalize on your God-given opportunity? If not, can you imagine Orpah having to live with the fact that she forfeited the opportunity to be in the lineage of the Messiah, like Ruth?

I would be derelict if I did not mention that the Lord called Moses when he was shepherding his father-in-law's livestock. God also called two other prophets, David, and Amos, to His service while they were shepherding livestock (1 Samuel 16, Amos 7:14). The Lord calling shepherds to lead His people pointed to how Jesus, who is called the Good Shepherd, would lead people. David even communicated that the Lord was his Shepherd (Psalm 23:1). As the Good Shepherd, Jesus spoke of His willingness to leave ninety-nine sheep in the fold to search for and recover one lost sheep (Luke 15:1-7). The entirety of Luke chapter 15 is about God's willingness to accept sinners who repent. John chapter 10 addresses how Jesus relates to us just like how a shepherd does to his sheep, in terms of communication and protection. And in Matthew 25:31-46, Jesus spoke of Himself returning as a King, but, in judgment, like a shepherd, He will separate the sheep from the goats. Therefore, we cannot overlook the prophetic significance of what Moses was doing when the Lord called him to His service. On that note, let us now return to Moses at the burning bush.

After Moses asked the Lord to send someone else, God became angry with Moses (Exodus 4:14). The Lord offered to have Moses's brother, Aaron, accompany him on his assignment to speak to the pharaoh of Egypt. Intriguingly, why didn't the Lord simply give Aaron or someone else the assignment? But clearly, upon examining the circumstances around Moses's birth, the Lord had brought him into the world for a purpose, His divine purpose (Exodus 1-2). It is like when the Lord called a young man named Jeremiah as a prophet and He said:

The Prophet's Life

Before I formed thee in the belly I knew thee; and before thou camest forth out of the womb I sanctified thee, and I ordained thee a prophet unto the nations.
~ Jeremiah 1:5

That points to the fact that the Lord God ordains people as prophets before they are born or even conceived. Another such example is what Gabriel prophesied about the birth of John the Baptist (Luke 1:13-17). If Moses was not going to fulfill the purpose for which God had created and sent him, then what purpose would he have served on the earth?

In a book about prophetic fACTS and acts, how could I have skipped by the miracles of the Lord turning Moses's rod into a serpent and then back into a rod, and later making his hand leprous and then normal again? There are many miraculous things about Moses's ministry that I will not cover, such as the ten plagues he called down on Egypt, the parting of the Red Sea, and the two occasions when the Lord used him to make water flow from two rocks in the wilderness. That is because this book is about how things in a prophet's life may be prophetic, even though everything about a prophet's life is not prophetic.

When Moses finally accepted his calling from God, and it seemed as if the Lord was pleased with him, things took a turn for the worse when the following unfolded:

At a lodging place on the way the Lord met him **and sought to put him to death.**
Then Zipporah took a flint and cut off her son's foreskin and touched Moses' feet with it and said, "Surely you are a bridegroom of blood to me!"
So He let him alone.
It was then that she said, "A bridegroom of blood," because of the circumcision. ~ Exodus 4:24-26 (ESV)

The Prophet's Life

Moses exercised his free will, and it almost got him killed. It was a prophetic act of intercession for Zipporah to immediately circumcise their son and use the prepuce to touch Moses's feet. Zipporah's actions pointed back to when the Lord made a covenant with Abram and told him that his children would be in captivity for 400 years, but He would deliver them (Genesis 15). It was time for the Lord to fulfill His promise to His friend Abram/Abraham. Also, Moses's wife saved his life because she reminded God of His covenant of circumcision with Abraham, and through Isaac (Genesis 18). So, thanks to Moses's wife, and her prophetic acts, the Lord had mercy on Moses.

The way the Lord handled Moses was not limited to him. Later, when the Lord told Balaam not to go with Balak's men, he obeyed. When Balak sent another contingent of men, the Lord's initial answer still applied. But after Balaam asked again, the Lord allowed him to go with them. Yet, when Balaam was traveling with Balak's men, in obedience to the Lord, God's anger was kindled against him. Therefore, the angel of the Lord stood in the way to kill Balaam (Numbers 22:22-35). The Lord had mercy on Balaam but constrained his actions. That mandate and divine constraint still apply to prophets.

In another example of a prophet trying to exercise his free will, Jonah knowingly and openly defied God. The Lord had commanded Jonah to go east to preach at Nineveh, but Jonah boarded a ship to set sail westward to Tarshish. Things went well for Jonah for a while, even to the point where he dozed off on the ship while in his disobedience to the Lord. Jonah soon found out that he was on a short leash when the Lord disturbed his peace in the ensuing events:

> But the Lord sent out a great wind into the sea, and there was a mighty tempest in the sea, so that the ship was like to be broken.

The Prophet's Life

Then the mariners were afraid, and cried every man unto his god, and cast forth the wares that were in the ship into the sea, to lighten it of them... ~ Jonah 1:4-5

Surprisingly, in his disobedience to the Lord, Jonah later remarked that he feared God (Jonah 1:9). But that alleged fear did not constrain the prophet from temporarily disobeying the Lord. Jonah's story did not end with the sailors simply casting him overboard and a great fish swallowing him. There are two prophetic angles to that part of the story. The first is that Jonah was in the fish's belly for three days and three nights. As Jesus said, that incident became a prophetic act to show what would happen to Him after His death and burial, and how He would be resurrected:

An evil and adulterous generation seeks for a sign, but no sign will be given to it except the **sign of the Prophet Jonah**.
For just as Jonah was three days and three nights in the belly of the great fish, so will the Son of Man be three days and three nights in the heart of the earth.
The men of Nineveh will rise up at the judgment with this generation and condemn it, for they repented at the preaching of Jonah, and behold, something greater than Jonah is here. ~ Matthew 12:39-41

The second prophetic angle of Jonah's ordeal is that he disobeyed the Lord. As a result, Jonah's smooth sailing life turned tumultuous before the sailors cast him into the sea where he ended up in the fish's belly. Likewise, for those who refuse to serve the Lord. He will not force them to love and serve Him, but their rejection either could or will cause them to get tossed into hell and subsequently into the lake of fire and brimstone.

Jonah's descent into the sea and the fish's belly is a prophetic act that points to this prophecy:

The Prophet's Life

Therefore hell hath enlarged herself, and opened her mouth without measure: and their glory, and their multitude, and their pomp, and he that rejoiceth, shall descend into it. *And the mean man shall be brought down, and the mighty man shall be humbled, and the eyes of the lofty shall be humbled: But the Lord of hosts shall be exalted in judgment, and God that is holy shall be sanctified in righteousness.*
~ Isaiah 5:14-16

Like a great fish, hell enlarges herself to receive the rebellious who will descend into her belly. One day, hell will repeat the fish's prophetic act by regurgitating those whom she had swallowed so Jesus can judge them (Revelation 20:13).

The above references to hell may seem extreme. But being cast into the Mediterranean Sea and getting swallowed by the fish was the beginning of what taught Jonah, a prophet of the Lord, to truly fear God. He also learned that his assignment was not a request. As Jonah stated, he had a taste of hell that prompted his repentance and obedience:

Then Jonah prayed unto the Lord his God out of the fish's belly, and said, I cried by reason of mine affliction unto the Lord, and He heard me; ***out of the belly of hell cried I****, and Thou heardest my voice.*
For Thou hadst cast me into the deep, in the midst of the seas; and the floods compassed me about: all thy billows and thy waves passed over me.
Then I said, I am cast out of Thy sight; yet I will look again toward Thy holy Temple.
The waters compassed me about, even to the soul: the depth closed me round about, the weeds were wrapped about my head. I went down to the bottoms of the mountains; the earth with her bars was about me for ever: yet hast Thou brought up my life from corruption, O Lord my God.

The Prophet's Life

When my soul fainted within me I remembered the Lord: and my prayer came in unto Thee, into Thine holy Temple. They that observe lying vanities forsake their own mercy. But I will sacrifice unto Thee with the voice of thanksgiving; I will pay that that I have vowed. Salvation is of the Lord.
And the Lord spake unto the fish, and it vomited out Jonah upon the dry land. ~ Jonah 2

Subsequently, when the Lord repeated His command to Jonah to go to Nineveh, he obeyed (Jonah 3). The prophet complained to the Lord about how He handled the situation by allowing the repentant Ninevites to live after he had prophesied to them, but Jonah did not dare disobey the Lord again. Jonah's story shows that whatever free will a person has, God is in control of the circumstances that impacts the person's decisions. It is also written:

The king's heart is in the hand of the Lord, as the rivers of water: He turneth it whithersoever He will.
~ Proverbs 21:1

I close this subsection about Jonah with this interesting and positive prophetic fACT. When Jonah prophesied to the Ninevites, as is recorded in the Scripture, he defied prophetic convention. While other prophets throughout the Bible gave the Word of the Lord by indicating that it came from an angel, Holy Spirit, or God the Father, Jonah simply said:

Yet forty days, and Nineveh shall be overthrown.
~ Jonah 3:4

The people had to discern that Jonah was speaking on the Lord's behalf. But, to Jonah's credit, his prophetic utterance earmarked how Jesus would prophesy. Jesus simply spoke without saying the Lord said, because He

The Prophet's Life

was the Lord. This is an example of one such prophecy from Jesus:

> *And He said, I tell thee, Peter, the cock shall not crow this day, before that thou shalt thrice deny that thou knowest Me.* ~ Luke 22:34

It is important for people to know that every prophecy will not have the vernacular to indicate that the Lord is communicating. Some things must be spiritually discerned. After His resurrection, when Jesus walked with two of His disciples on the road to Emmaus, they did not recognize His form. However, they reported that their hearts burned within them as He opened the Scriptures unto them (Luke 24:13-35). That burning is reminiscent of what Jeremiah experienced when he tried to abstain from releasing the Word of the Lord (Jeremiah 20:7-9).

Regarding discerning when the Lord is using someone to communicate, without specifying that He directed that person to speak, a fitting example is found in the life of David. After Nabal had disrespected him, and David had gathered his men to confront Nabal, when Abigail, Nabal's wife found out, she went to intercede on her family's behalf. As a result of her actions, David said to her:

> **Blessed be the Lord God of Israel, which sent thee this day to meet me:** *And blessed be thy advice, and blessed be thou, which hast kept me this day from coming to shed blood, and from avenging myself with mine own hand.*
> *For in very deed, as the Lord God of Israel liveth, which hath kept me back from hurting thee, except thou hadst hasted and come to meet me, surely there had not been left unto Nabal by the morning light any that pisseth against the wall.* ~ 1 Samuel 25:32-34

David made that statement even though Abigail never said the Lord sent her. As a CHRISTian, it is important to

The Prophet's Life

discern when the Lord is communicating to you, and that includes when He is either speaking TO or THROUGH another person.

Like Jonah and other prophets, Moses also complained to the Lord about things. One such instance serves as a prophetic act. After the Lord had used Moses to deliver the children of Israel out of Egypt, they started lusting for some of the perceived benefits they had in captivity. They had grown tired of being in the wilderness subsisting on manna instead of the variety of foods they had in Egypt, then these things happened:

> *Then Moses heard the people weep throughout their families, every man in the door of his tent: and the anger of the Lord was kindled greatly; Moses also was displeased.*
>
> *And Moses said unto the Lord,* **Wherefore hast Thou afflicted Thy servant? And wherefore have I not found favour in Thy sight, that Thou layest the burden of all this people upon me?**
>
> *Have I conceived all this people? Have I begotten them, that Thou shouldest say unto me, Carry them in thy bosom, as a nursing father beareth the sucking child, unto the land which Thou swarest unto their fathers?*
>
> *Whence should I have flesh to give unto all this people? For they weep unto me, saying, Give us flesh, that we may eat.*
>
> **I am not able to bear all this people alone, because it is too heavy for me.**
>
> *And if Thou deal thus with me, kill me, I pray Thee, out of hand, if I have found favour in Thy sight; and let me not see my wretchedness.*
>
> *And the Lord said unto Moses, Gather unto me seventy men of the elders of Israel, whom thou knowest to be the elders of the people, and officers over them; and bring them unto the tabernacle of the congregation, that they may stand there with thee. And I will come down and talk with thee there:* **and I will take of the Spirit**

The Prophet's Life

which is upon thee, and will put it upon them; *and they shall bear the burden of the people with thee, that thou bear it not thyself alone.* ~ Numbers 11:10-17

After the Lord removed some of His Holy Spirit from Moses, and He rested on the seventy elders, they prophesied as a sign of receiving the Holy Spirit. Two of the men, Eldad and Medad, had remained in the camp but still prophesied upon receiving the Holy Spirit. When the news came out of the camp, Joshua's protest resulted in Moses making an interesting statement:

And Joshua the son of Nun, the servant of Moses, one of his young men, answered and said, My lord Moses, forbid them.
And Moses said unto him, Enviest thou for my sake? Would God that all the Lord's people were prophets, and that the Lord would put His Spirit upon them!
~ Numbers 11:28-29

Moses's brother and sister, Aaron, and Miriam, were prophets, yet the only person the Lord removed a measure of His Spirit from was Moses (Numbers 12:1; Exodus 7:1, 15:20). That points to how John the Baptist said God had given Jesus the Holy Spirit without measure (John 3:34). Jesus later told His disciples that it was expedient for Him to leave so the Comforter, the Holy Spirit, would come unto them (John 16:7). Prior to His ascension back into heaven, Jesus said:

But ye shall receive power, after that the Holy Ghost is come upon you: and ye shall be witnesses unto Me both in Jerusalem, and in all Judaea, and in Samaria, and unto the uttermost part of the earth. ~ Acts 11:8

They received that power ten days later, on the Day of Pentecost, when the Holy Spirit descended on the earth

The Prophet's Life

as a rushing mighty wind. Some onlookers claimed the disciples were under the influence of wine, until this:

> *But Peter, standing up with the eleven, lifted up his voice, and said unto them, Ye men of Judaea, and all ye that dwell at Jerusalem, be this known unto you, and hearken to my words: For these are not drunken, as ye suppose, seeing it is but the third hour of the day.*
> *But this is that which was spoken by the prophet Joel;* **And it shall come to pass in the last days, saith God, I will pour out of My Spirit upon all flesh: and your sons and your daughters shall prophesy, and your young men shall see visions, and**
> **And on My servants and on My handmaidens I will pour out in those days of My Spirit; and they shall prophesy:** *And I will shew wonders in heaven above, and signs in the earth beneath; blood, and fire, and vapour of smoke: The sun shall be turned into darkness, and the moon into blood, before the great and notable day of the Lord come: And it shall come to pass, that whosoever shall call on the name of the Lord shall be saved.* ~ Acts 2:14-21

Peter referred to what Joel had prophesied as recorded in Joel 2:28-31. But what Peter and Joel stated point back to when Moses said he would have loved if all the Lord's children were prophets. Even though a person who prophesies may not be a prophet, the outpouring of the Lord's Spirit, to the point where all Believers may prophesy, whether they realise it or not, is in keeping with Moses's desire.

So, to recap, Moses had a large measure of God's Spirit, even to the point where some of Him was removed from Moses and conferred upon others. Likewise, Jesus, who had the Holy Spirit beyond measure, said it was good for Him to go (back to heaven) so that Believers could receive the Holy Spirit in a greater dispensation.

The Prophet's Life

Another of Moses's prophetic acts was to stand in the gap for Israel, despite their (continued) rebellion against God. Moses was with the Lord when the Israelites built a golden calf and started worshipping it. Their actions caught God's attention and incurred His wrath, until Moses interceded for them, like how Jesus does for us:

> *And the Lord said unto Moses, Go, get thee down; for thy people, which thou broughtest out of the land of Egypt, have corrupted themselves: They have turned aside quickly out of the way which I commanded them: they have made them a molten calf, and have worshipped it, and have sacrificed thereunto, and said, These be thy gods, O Israel, which have brought thee up out of the land of Egypt.*
>
> *And the Lord said unto Moses, I have seen this people, and, behold, it is a stiffnecked people: Now therefore let Me alone, that My wrath may wax hot against them, and that I may consume them: and I will make of thee a great nation.*
>
> *And Moses besought the Lord his God, and said, Lord, why doth Thy wrath wax hot against Thy people, which Thou hast brought forth out of the land of Egypt with great power, and with a mighty hand?*
>
> *Wherefore should the Egyptians speak, and say, For mischief did He bring them out, to slay them in the mountains, and to consume them from the face of the earth?*
>
> *Turn from Thy fierce wrath, and repent of this evil against Thy people.*
>
> *Remember Abraham, Isaac, and Israel, Thy servants, to whom Thou swarest by Thine own self, and saidst unto them, I will multiply your seed as the stars of heaven, and all this land that I have spoken of will I give unto your seed, and they shall inherit it for ever.*
>
> *And the Lord repented of the evil which He thought to do unto His people.* ~ Exodus 32:7-14

The Prophet's Life

If we only knew how many times Jesus stood in the gap like that to intercede on our behalf...

Time for another **"Praise Break!!!"**

But that was not the end of Moses's prophetic acts during that time. This marks another significant one:

And it came to pass, as soon as he came nigh unto the camp, that he saw the calf, and the dancing: and Moses' anger waxed hot, and he cast the tables out of his hands, and brake them beneath the mount.
And he took the calf which they had made, and burnt it in the fire, and ground it to powder, and strawed it upon the water, and made the children of Israel drink of it.
~ Exodus 32:19-20

The Israelites had already received the Ten Commandments before they were written in stone (Exodus 20). Under the Old Covenant, and the Law of Moses, many of the things were physical. According to the New Covenant, the Commandments are written on our hearts instead of on stone. Now the Holy Spirit convicts us when we are on the verge of breaking the Lord's Commandments, for which we should listen and obey. When Moses physically broke the tablets with the Ten Commandments, it was a prophetic act to show the Israelites how they had broken the Lord's Commandments. Even his burning of the golden calf was a prophetic act to show how satan will be burned in everlasting fire, and those who worship him will partake in his judgment (Revelation 20:10-15).

Moses also did another prophetic act, which, when compared to the other things the Lord had used him to do, may not have seemed significant at all. It involved this other case of the wandering Israelites complaining about the Lord's provisions in the wilderness:

The Prophet's Life

And the people spake against God, and against Moses, Wherefore have ye brought us up out of Egypt to die in the wilderness? For there is no bread, neither is there any water; **and our soul loatheth this light bread.**
And the Lord sent fiery serpents among the people, and they bit the people; and much people of Israel died.
Therefore the people came to Moses, and said, We have sinned, for we have spoken against the Lord, and against thee; pray unto the Lord, that He take away the serpents from us.
And Moses prayed for the people.
And the Lord said unto Moses, Make thee a fiery serpent, and set it upon a pole: and it shall come to pass, that every one that is bitten, when he looketh upon it, shall live.
And Moses made a serpent of brass, and put it upon a pole, and it came to pass, that if a serpent had bitten any man, when he beheld the serpent of brass, he lived.
~ Numbers 21:5-9

Again, Moses interceded for the people like how Jesus intercedes for us. Jesus addressed the above circumstances on two separate occasions. In this first one, the Lord spoke of why it was so offensive that the people had despised the manna, which foreshadowed how people would hate Him:

And when they had found Him on the other side of the sea, they said unto Him, Rabbi, when camest Thou hither?
Jesus answered them and said, Verily, verily, I say unto you, Ye seek Me, not because ye saw the miracles, but because ye did eat of the loaves, and were filled. **Labour not for the meat which perisheth, but for that meat which endureth unto everlasting life, which the Son of Man shall give unto you: for Him hath God the Father sealed.**

The Prophet's Life

Then said they unto Him, What shall we do, that we might work the works of God?
Jesus answered and said unto them, This is the work of God, that ye believe on Him whom He hath sent.
They said therefore unto Him, What sign shewest Thou then, that we may see, and believe Thee? What dost Thou work? Our fathers did eat manna in the desert; as it is written, He gave them bread from heaven to eat.
Then Jesus said unto them, ***Verily, verily, I say unto you, Moses gave you not that bread from heaven; but My Father giveth you the True Bread from heaven. For the Bread of God is He which cometh down from heaven, and giveth life unto the world.***
Then said they unto Him, Lord, evermore give us this Bread.
And Jesus said unto them, ***I AM the Bread of Life:*** *he that cometh to Me shall never hunger; and he that believeth on Me shall never thirst.*
But I said unto you, That ye also have seen Me, and believe not.
All that the Father giveth Me shall come to Me; and him that cometh to Me I will in no wise cast out. ***For I came down from heaven, NOT TO DO MINE OWN WILL, BUT THE WILL OF HIM THAT SENT ME.***
And this is the ***Father's will which hath sent Me****, that of all which He hath given Me I should lose nothing, but should raise it up again at the last day.*
And this is the ***will of Him that sent Me****, that every one which seeth the Son, and believeth on Him, may have everlasting life: and I will raise him up at the last day.*
The Jews then murmured at Him, because He said, ***I AM the Bread which came down from heaven.***
~ John 6:25-41

Prior to the above, Jesus had performed a prophetic act by feeding five thousand men, not to mention women and children, with five barley loaves of bread and two small

The Prophet's Life

fish. In another case, He used seven loaves of bread and a few small fish to feed four thousand men, plus the women and children. Scriptures specify that Jesus blessed the bread and then broke them to feed the masses (Mark 6:41, Matthew 15:29-39). Both were symbolic of how Jesus would give up His body and life for the world. And in keeping with His Words in John 6, at what we refer to as "The Last Supper," Jesus's prophetic act of blessing the bread pointed back to establishing the Old Covenant with Moses and the sustaining power of the manna in the wilderness. Jesus's actions also pointed to how He, the Manna, would sustain us in the future:

> *And as they were eating, Jesus took bread, and blessed it, and brake it, and gave it to the disciples, and said, Take, eat; this is My body.*
> *And He took the cup, and gave thanks, and gave it to them, saying, Drink ye all of it; For this is My blood of the New Testament, which is shed for many for the remission of sins. ~ Matthew 26:26-28*

In addition, Jesus also specified how Moses's prophetic act in Numbers 21 was a prelude to what He would do, and its significance, when He said to Nicodemus:

> **And as Moses lifted up the serpent in the wilderness, even so must the Son of Man be lifted up:** *That whosoever believeth in Him should not perish, but have eternal life.*
> *For God so loved the world, that He gave His only begotten Son, that whosoever believeth in Him should not perish, but have everlasting life. For God sent not His Son into the world to condemn the world; but that the world through Him might be saved. He that believeth on Him is not condemned: but he that believeth not is condemned already, because he hath not believed in the name of the only begotten Son of God. ~ John 3:14-18*

The Prophet's Life

To add to its prophetic significance, the Lord reiterated a part of that later in His life and ministry:

Now is the judgment of this world: now shall the prince of this world be cast out.
And I, if I be lifted up from the earth, will draw all men unto me.
This He said, signifying what death He should die.
~ John 12:31-33

We can learn another lesson from what the Lord said to Nicodemus. Ever since the events in Genesis 3, the serpent has had a bad reputation. Consequently, sometimes we can make hasty generalizations by classifying some things as being always bad or even always good. Certainly, the devil and his angels are always evil, and God is always good. But there are other things we may not correctly discern. For example, a serpent is not always inherently bad. Aaron's rod turned into a serpent, and it swallowed the Egyptian magicians' serpents. Moses made a brass serpent to counteract the venom of the snakes. Jesus spoke of sending out His disciples as sheep among wolves, but they should be as wise as serpents and harmless as doves (Matthew 10:16). And then Jesus spoke of Himself being a source of salvation when He is raised like a serpent. Those analogies indicate that Jesus is the antivenin from the sting of death, about Whom it is written:

O death, where is thy sting? O grave, where is thy victory?
The sting of death is sin; and the strength of sin is the Law. ***But thanks be to God, which giveth us the victory through our Lord Jesus Christ.***
~ 1 Corinthians 15:55-57

Some things are a matter of perspective and/or who, such as which deity, is putting them to use. Sometimes

The Prophet's Life

there is a thin line between an omen and a prophetic act. Each person, with the help of the Holy Spirit, needs to discern the difference.

In closing, Moses's ministry was filled with many signs and wonders. But do not overlook the prophetic acts from his life, things that pointed to the character and deeds of the coming Messiah, Jesus, the Christ. It is also fair to clarify something about Moses regarding why he was such a reluctant prophet when the Lord called him. It was one of the last things the Lord addressed in His commissioning of Moses. A part of Moses's fear was rooted in his criminal history. He had killed an Egyptian in defense of his Hebrew brothers, which was why he fled from Egypt and lived in exile for forty years (Exodus 2:11-25). But the Lord reassured Moses that everyone who sought his life was dead (Exodus 4:19). Interestingly, as Stephen later articulated, even Moses's defense of his Hebrew brothers that resulted in the Egyptian's death was a prophetic sign:

> *And Moses was learned in all the wisdom of the Egyptians, and was mighty in words and in deeds.*
> *And when he was full forty years old, it came into his heart to visit his brethren the children of Israel.*
> *And seeing one of them suffer wrong, he defended him, and avenged him that was oppressed, and smote the Egyptian:* **For he supposed his brethren would have understood how that God by His hand would deliver them: but they understood not.**
> ~ Acts 7:22-25

CHAPTER 3
Ezekiel

And they,
whether they will hear, or whether they will forbear,
(for they are a rebellious house,) yet shall know
that there hath been a prophet among them.
~ Yahweh (Ezekiel 2:5)

The Lord used the ministry of Ezekiel to inspire this book, primarily based on this event in the prophet's life:

Also the Word of the Lord came unto me, saying, Son of man, behold, I take away from thee the desire of thine eyes with a stroke: yet neither shalt thou mourn nor weep, neither shall thy tears run down. Forbear to cry, make no mourning for the dead, bind the tire of thine head upon thee, and put on thy shoes upon thy feet, and cover not thy lips, and eat not the bread of men.
~ Ezekiel 24:15-17

What did the Lord mean by the desire of his eyes, for whom he should not mourn?

The Prophet's Life

We find out the painful truth behind that prophetic act as the story ensues:

> *So I spake unto the people in the morning:* **and at even my wife died;** *and I did in the morning as I was commanded.*
> *And the people said unto me, Wilt thou not tell us what these things are to us, that thou doest so?*
> *Then I answered them, The Word of the Lord came unto me, saying, Speak unto the house of Israel, Thus saith the Lord God; Behold, I will profane My sanctuary, the excellency of your strength,* **the desire of your eyes,** *and that which your soul pitieth; and your sons and your daughters whom ye have left shall fall by the sword.* **And ye shall do as I have done: ye shall not cover your lips, nor eat the bread of men. And your tires shall be upon your heads, and your shoes upon your feet: ye shall not mourn nor weep; but ye shall pine away for your iniquities, and mourn one toward another. THUS EZEKIEL IS UNTO YOU A SIGN: according to all that he hath done shall ye do: and when this cometh, ye shall know that I AM the Lord God.**
> *Also, thou son of man, shall it not be in the day when I take from them their strength, the joy of their glory,* **the desire of their eyes**, *and that whereupon they set their minds, their sons and their daughters, that he that escapeth in that day shall come unto thee, to cause thee to hear it with thine ears? In that day shall thy mouth be opened to him which is escaped, and thou shalt speak, and be no more dumb:* **and thou shalt be a sign unto them; and they shall know that I AM the Lord.**
> ~ Ezekiel 24:18-27

The Lord used Ezekiel as a sign unto the people, and not simply via his prophetic Words, but also and initially through his prophetic acts. The death of Ezekiel's wife, and his response to her passing, are also linked to other

The Prophet's Life

prophets, and how their marriages or things in their romantic relationships were also prophetic acts.

One such notable prophet is Hosea, whom the Lord told to marry a promiscuous woman, which was a prophetic act. Hosea married Gomer, but please note the prophetic implications of the children the Lord blessed them with:

So he went and took Gomer the daughter of Diblaim; which conceived, and bare him a son.
And the Lord said unto him, Call his name Jezreel; for yet a little while, and I will avenge the blood of Jezreel upon the house of Jehu, and will cause to cease the kingdom of the house of Israel. And it shall come to pass at that day, that I will break the bow of Israel, in the valley of Jezreel.
And she conceived again, and bare a daughter.
And God said unto him, Call her name Loruhamah: for I will no more have mercy upon the house of Israel; but I will utterly take them away. But I will have mercy upon the house of Judah, and will save them by the Lord their God, and will not save them by bow, nor by sword, nor by battle, by horses, nor by horsemen.
Now when she had weaned Loruhamah, she conceived, and bare a son.
Then said God, Call his name Loammi: for ye are not My people, and I will not be your God. Yet the number of the children of Israel shall be as the sand of the sea, which cannot be measured nor numbered; and it shall come to pass, that in the place where it was said unto them, Ye are not My people, there it shall be said unto them, Ye are the sons of the living God. Then shall the children of Judah and the children of Israel be gathered together, and appoint themselves one head, and they shall come up out of the land: for great shall be the day of Jezreel.
~ Hosea 1:3-11

They did not have the free will to name the children the Lord had blessed them with as they pleased. The Lord had

The Prophet's Life

a purpose for those children, so He called them by name. Prophets are servants of the Lord who serve Him at His pleasure. Therefore, while for some people, such actions may seem tyrannical, the Lord's prophets willingly submit to His divine constraints, even when it is not pleasurable to submit to their Master's will. Every child of God should realize that He knows what is best for them, even more than they could ever possibly know what is best for themselves. Armed with that bit of knowledge, it should be easier for God's children to submit to His will.

This other case shows that Hosea was not the only prophet who had such an experience in their service to the Lord their God:

Moreover the Lord said unto me, Take thee a great roll, and write in it with a man's pen concerning Mahershalalhashbaz.
And I took unto me faithful witnesses to record, Uriah the priest, and Zechariah the son of Jeberechiah.
And I went unto the prophetess; and she conceived, and bare a son.
Then said the Lord to me, Call his name Mahershalalhashbaz. For before the child shall have knowledge to cry, My father, and my mother, the riches of Damascus and the spoil of Samaria shall be taken away before the king of Assyria. ~ Isaiah 8:1-4

Many people would consider the above prophetic acts from Hosea and Isaiah easy in comparison to this one:

In the year that Tartan came unto Ashdod, (when Sargon the king of Assyria sent him,) and fought against Ashdod, and took it; At the same time spake the Lord by Isaiah the son of Amoz, saying, Go and loose the sackcloth from off thy loins, and put off thy shoe from thy foot.
And he did so, walking naked and barefoot.

The Prophet's Life

And the Lord said, **Like as My servant Isaiah hath walked naked and barefoot three years for a sign and wonder upon Egypt and upon Ethiopia**; *So shall the king of Assyria lead away the Egyptians prisoners, and the Ethiopians captives, young and old, naked and barefoot, even with their buttocks uncovered, to the shame of Egypt. And they shall be afraid and ashamed of Ethiopia their expectation, and of Egypt their glory. And the inhabitant of this isle shall say in that day, Behold, such is our expectation, whither we flee for help to be delivered from the king of Assyria: and how shall we escape?* ~ Isaiah 20

That was one of the most challenging prophetic acts in the Bible, but as the Lord said, it was for His divine purpose. In addition, when Isaiah walked around naked for three years, it is highly likely that his wife was still alive to support him during that time. So even a prophet's family is subject to being a part of God's prophetic acts.

The Lord told Hosea what kind of woman to marry and what to name their children, and what Isaiah should name his son. But the Lord gave the prophet Jeremiah a different set of instructions. Jeremiah's actions in obedience to the Lord could be classified as inactions, yet they would serve as a sign for Judah:

The Word of the Lord came also unto me, saying, **THOU SHALT NOT take thee a wife, neither SHALT THOU have sons or daughters IN THIS PLACE.**
For thus saith the Lord concerning the sons and concerning the daughters that are born in this place, and concerning their mothers that bare them, and concerning their fathers that begat them in this land; They shall die of grievous deaths; they shall not be lamented; neither shall they be buried; but they shall be as dung upon the face of the earth: and they shall be consumed by the sword, and by famine; and their carcases shall be meat for the fowls of heaven, and for the beasts of the earth.

The Prophet's Life

For thus saith the Lord, **Enter not into the house of mourning, neither go to lament nor bemoan them:** *for I have taken away My peace from this people, saith the Lord, even lovingkindness and mercies.*

Both the great and the small shall die in this land: they shall not be buried, neither shall men lament for them, nor cut themselves, nor make themselves bald for them: Neither shall men tear themselves for them in mourning, to comfort them for the dead; neither shall men give them the cup of consolation to drink for their father or for their mother.

Thou shalt not also go into the house of feasting, to sit with them to eat and to drink.

For thus saith the Lord of Hosts, the God of Israel; Behold, I will cause to cease out of this place in your eyes, and in your days, the voice of mirth, and the voice of gladness, the voice of the bridegroom, and the voice of the bride.

And it shall come to pass, when thou shalt shew this people all these Words, and they shall say unto thee, Wherefore hath the Lord pronounced all this great evil against us? Or what is our iniquity? Or what is our sin that we have committed against the Lord our God?

Then shalt thou say unto them, Because your fathers have forsaken Me, saith the Lord, and have walked after other gods, and have served them, and have worshipped them, and have forsaken Me, and have not kept My Law; And ye have done worse than your fathers; for, behold, ye walk every one after the imagination of his evil heart, that they may not hearken unto Me: Therefore will I cast you out of this land into a land that ye know not, neither ye nor your fathers; and there shall ye serve other gods day and night; where I will not shew you favour.

Therefore, behold, the days come, saith the Lord, that it shall no more be said, The Lord liveth, that brought up the children of Israel out of the land of Egypt; But, The Lord liveth, that brought up the children of Israel

The Prophet's Life

from the land of the north, and from all the lands whither he had driven them: and I will bring them again into their land that I gave unto their fathers.
Behold, I will send for many fishers, saith the Lord, and they shall fish them; and after will I send for many hunters, and they shall hunt them from every mountain, and from every hill, and out of the holes of the rocks. For Mine eyes are upon all their ways: they are not hid from My face, neither is their iniquity hid from Mine eyes. And first I will recompense their iniquity and their sin double; because they have defiled My land, they have filled Mine inheritance with the carcases of their detestable and abominable things.
O Lord, my strength, and my fortress, and my refuge in the day of affliction, the Gentiles shall come unto thee from the ends of the earth, and shall say, Surely our fathers have inherited lies, vanity, and things wherein there is no profit.
Shall a man make gods unto himself, and they are no gods?
Therefore, behold, I will this once cause them to know, I will cause them to know Mine hand and My might; and they shall know that My name is The Lord.
~ Jeremiah 16

That was not to say Jeremiah could nEVER get married, only that he was not allowed to marry any of the women in that place and have children with them. It was like when Abraham sent his servant to find a wife for Isaac but said the woman could not be a Canaanite (Genesis 24:1-4). In Jeremiah's case, IF he had disobeyed the Lord and married a Judean, not even his relationship with that woman would have saved her from God's judgment. In fact, IF he had disobeyed the Lord and gotten married at that time, it would have imperiled him.

Now back to Hosea who experienced some marital problems when his wife Gomer entered a relationship with another man. Even though they had not gotten

The Prophet's Life

divorced, this aspect of the Law of Moses points to it being abominable for Hosea to rekindle his relationship with Gomer:

> *...And when she is departed out of his house, she may go and be another man's wife.*
> *And if the latter husband hate her, and write her a bill of divorcement, and giveth it in her hand, and sendeth her out of his house; or if the latter husband die, which took her to be his wife;* **Her former husband, which sent her away, may not take her again to be his wife, AFTER THAT SHE IS DEFILED; FOR THAT IS ABOMINATION BEFORE THE LORD:** *and thou shalt not cause the land to sin, which the Lord thy God giveth thee for an inheritance.* ~ Deuteronomy 24:2-4

However, the Lord did not instruct Hosea to cut off Gomer. Instead, the Lord's instructions were more akin to what happened with another prophet, King David. The intolerable life-threatening conditions in King Saul's house caused David to flee and leave his wife, Saul's daughter, Michal, behind. Despite no evidence of David's death, Saul gave Michal to Phalti/Phaltiel as his wife (1 Samuel 25:44). Years later, after Saul's death, when David was king of Hebron, and on the verge of becoming king over Israel, despite having married other women, he demanded to have his first wife back. One of the things David mentioned in his demand was that he had paid a price for his bride (2 Samuel 3:12-16). David had to risk his life for the opportunity to marry Michal. That is something Phaltiel most certainly did not have to do, and especially to the extent that David did. In fact, Saul used the prospects of marriage to try to get David killed (1 Samuel 18:17-29).

David paid a price for Michal, and likewise, Hosea had to pay a price to redeem Gomer:

The Prophet's Life

Then said the Lord unto me, Go yet, love a woman beloved of her friend, yet an adulteress, according to the love of the Lord toward the children of Israel, who look to other gods, and love flagons of wine.
So I bought her to me for fifteen pieces of silver, and for an homer of barley, and an half homer of barley: And I said unto her, Thou shalt abide for me many days; thou shalt not play the harlot, and thou shalt not be for another man: so will I also be for thee.
For the children of Israel shall abide many days without a king, and without a prince, and without a sacrifice, and without an image, and without an ephod, and without teraphim: Afterward shall the children of Israel return, and seek the Lord their God, and David their king; and shall fear the Lord and his goodness in the latter days. ~ Hosea 3

The Scripture points to the greater significance of Hosea's prophetic act to redeem Gomer. It was demonstrative of God's love for Israel, and how, despite her adulterous ways towards Him, He was willing to pay the price to redeem her. God considered Israel serving other gods as "spiritual adultery," particularly based on this remark:

For thy Maker is thine Husband; *the Lord of Hosts is His name; and thy Redeemer the Holy One of Israel; The God of the whole earth shall He be called. ~ Isaiah 54:5*

In keeping with the Spirit of Prophecy as told in Revelation 19:10, the events in Hosea 3 also point to Jesus, the Christ. He was the Husband whom God sent to Israel, and most of the Israelites rejected Him (John 1:10-11). But Jesus still paid a price for them. So, like David, who had many wives but still wanted his first wife returned to him, the Gentiles in large part accepted Jesus as their Husband, but He still wants His Jewish bride. But because of Israel's rejection of Jesus as her Husband,

The Prophet's Life

she will end up in the arms of another husband, the Antichrist. Only then will Israel wholeheartedly wake up to the truth of who her Husband is. Yet, like Hosea, the Lord will return for His bride, for whom He paid a price when He sacrificed His life for her. That is also linked to when the Lord said to the prophet:

> *They say, If a man put away his wife, and she go from him, and become another man's, shall he return unto her again? Shall not that land be greatly polluted? But thou hast played the harlot with many lovers;* **YET RETURN AGAIN TO ME, saith the Lord.**
> *Lift up thine eyes unto the high places, and see where thou hast not been lien with. In the ways hast thou sat for them, as the Arabian in the wilderness; and thou hast polluted the land with thy whoredoms and with thy wickedness.*
> *Therefore the showers have been withholden, and there hath been no latter rain; and thou hadst a whore's forehead, thou refusedst to be ashamed.*
> *Wilt thou not from this time cry unto Me, My father, thou art the guide of my youth?*
> *Will He reserve His anger for ever? Will He keep it to the end? Behold, thou hast spoken and done evil things as thou couldest.*
> *The Lord said also unto me in the days of Josiah the king, Hast thou seen that which backsliding Israel hath done? She is gone up upon every high mountain and under every green tree, and there hath played the harlot.* **And I said after she had done all these things, TURN THOU UNTO ME. But she returned not.** *And her treacherous sister Judah saw it.*
> **And I saw, when for all the causes whereby BACKSLIDING ISRAEL COMMITTED ADULTERY I had put her away, and given her a bill of divorce; yet her treacherous sister Judah feared not, but went and played the harlot also.**

The Prophet's Life

And it came to pass through the lightness of her whoredom, that she defiled the land, and committed adultery with stones and with stocks.
And yet for all this her treacherous sister JUDAH HATH NOT TURNED UNTO ME with her whole heart, but feignedly, saith the Lord.
And the Lord said unto me, The backsliding Israel hath justified herself more than treacherous Judah.
Go and proclaim these Words toward the north, and say, Return, thou backsliding Israel, saith the Lord; and I will not cause Mine anger to fall upon you: for I AM merciful, saith the Lord, and I will not keep anger for ever. Only acknowledge thine iniquity, that thou hast transgressed against the Lord thy God, and hast scattered thy ways to the strangers under every green tree, and ye have not obeyed My voice, saith the Lord.
Turn, O backsliding children, saith the Lord; ***for I AM married unto you:*** *and I will take you one of a city, and two of a family, and I will bring you to Zion: And I will give you pastors according to Mine heart, which shall feed you with knowledge and understanding.*
~ Jeremiah 3:1-15

The Lord views His relationship with Israel as a marriage, which communicates the depths of Jesus later rebuking certain messengers by saying He never knew them (Matthew 7:21-23). Despite having justification to permanently put away His wayward bride, the Lord was and is willing to take her back, IF she would only repent of her transgressions. Therefore, it should not come as a surprise that the relationship between prophets/prophetesses and their spouses may have prophetic implications regarding how people relate to the Lord, and how He relates to His people.

By God's grace, Ezekiel did the seemingly impossible in how he conducted himself after his wife's passing. But that would not be his only prophetic act. Ezekiel's prophetic ministry was filled with visionary experiences

The Prophet's Life

and other encounters with the Lord and His angels. But even from the infancy of his ministry, the Lord used Ezekiel to perform prophetic acts, first among them includes these:

> *And the hand of the Lord was there upon me; and He said unto me, Arise, go forth into the plain, and I will there talk with thee.*
> *Then I arose, and went forth into the plain: and, behold, the glory of the Lord stood there, as the glory which I saw by the river of Chebar: and I fell on my face.*
> *Then the Spirit entered into me, and set me upon my feet, and spake with me, and said unto me,* **Go, shut thyself within thine house.**
> *But thou, O son of man, behold, they shall put bands upon thee, and shall bind thee with them, and thou shalt not go out among them:* **And I WILL MAKE THY TONGUE CLEAVE TO THE ROOF OF THY MOUTH, that thou shalt be dumb, and shalt not be to them a reprover: for they are a rebellious house.**
> **But when I speak with thee, I WILL OPEN THY MOUTH, and thou shalt say unto them, Thus saith the Lord God;** *He that heareth, let him hear; and he that forbeareth, let him forbear: for they are a rebellious house.* ~ Ezekiel 3:22-27

Just imagine if [contemporary] prophets only spoke (prophesied) when the Lord commanded them to speak. Ezekiel's prophecies were prophetic acts, but so was his silence, particularly when the Lord restrained him.

As was the case with King Saul, it is an ominous sign when the Lord's prophets are silent. After years of rebellion that led to the Lord cutting him off, shortly before his death, King Saul inquired of the Lord. But, as it is written, the Lord did not answer him by dreams, Urim or by Prophets (1 Samuel 28:6). It was the proverbial quiet before the storm. Jesus also did that when He remained quiet while the Pharisees tried to entrap Him with the

The Prophet's Life

woman who had allegedly been caught in the act of committing adultery (John 8:1-11). More on this later...

The next chapter of the Book of the Prophet Ezekiel has him performing more prophetic acts for the glory of the Lord his God:

> *Thou also, son of man, take thee a tile, and lay it before thee, and pourtray upon it the city, even Jerusalem: And lay siege against it, and build a fort against it, and cast a mount against it; set the camp also against it, and set battering rams against it round about.*
>
> *Moreover take thou unto thee an iron pan, and set it for a wall of iron between thee and the city: and set thy face against it, and it shall be besieged, and thou shalt lay siege against it.* **This shall be a sign to the house of Israel.**
>
> **Lie thou also upon thy left side, and lay the iniquity of the house of Israel upon it:** *according to the number of the days that thou shalt lie upon it thou shalt bear their iniquity. For I have laid upon thee the years of their iniquity, according to the number of the days, three hundred and ninety days: so shalt thou bear the iniquity of the house of Israel.*
>
> **And when thou hast accomplished them, lie again on thy right side, and thou shalt bear the iniquity of the house of Judah forty days: I have appointed thee each day for a year.**
>
> *Therefore thou shalt set thy face toward the siege of Jerusalem, and thine arm shall be uncovered, and thou shalt prophesy against it.*
>
> *And, behold, I will lay bands upon thee, and thou shalt not turn thee from one side to another, till thou hast ended the days of thy siege.*
>
> *Take thou also unto thee wheat, and barley, and beans, and lentiles, and millet, and fitches, and put them in one vessel, and make thee bread thereof, according to the number of the days that thou shalt lie upon thy side, three hundred and ninety days shalt thou eat thereof.*

The Prophet's Life

And thy meat which thou shalt eat shall be by weight, twenty shekels a day: from time to time shalt thou eat it. Thou shalt drink also water by measure, the sixth part of an hin: from time to time shalt thou drink.
And thou shalt eat it as barley cakes, and thou shalt bake it with dung that cometh out of man, in their sight. And the Lord said, Even thus shall the children of Israel eat their defiled bread among the Gentiles, whither I will drive them.
Then said I, Ah Lord God! Behold, my soul hath not been polluted: for from my youth up even till now have I not eaten of that which dieth of itself, or is torn in pieces; neither came there abominable flesh into my mouth.
Then He said unto me, Lo, I have given thee cow's dung for man's dung, and thou shalt prepare thy bread therewith.
Moreover He said unto me, Son of man, behold, I will break the staff of bread in Jerusalem: and they shall eat bread by weight, and with care; and they shall drink water by measure, and with astonishment: That they may want bread and water, and be astonied one with another, and consume away for their iniquity.
~ Ezekiel 4

Note that Ezekiel did not exercise his free will by telling the Lord that he would not do as He had commanded. His only pushback was to beseech the Lord to not let him eat defiled foods, for which the Lord obliged. With the above example, and that of Isaiah walking around naked for three years, it makes me wonder if seeing some insane (looking) and/or homeless people could be some of the Lord's prophets performing prophetic acts for His glory. Perhaps you do not believe that the Lord has prophets today, which means those insane (looking) and/or homeless people could not be prophets. If that is the case, then please consider this:

The Prophet's Life

Let brotherly love continue.
Be not forgetful to entertain strangers: for thereby some have entertained angels unawares.
Remember them that are in bonds, as bound with them; and them which suffer adversity, as being yourselves also in the body. ~ Hebrews 13:1-3

It is also important to remember when Jesus said:

When the Son of Man shall come in His glory, and all the holy angels with Him, then shall He sit upon the throne of His glory: And before Him shall be gathered all nations: and He shall separate them one from another, as a shepherd divideth his sheep from the goats: And He shall set the sheep on His right hand, but the goats on the left.
Then shall the King say unto them on His right hand, Come, ye blessed of My Father, inherit the KINGdom prepared for you from the foundation of the world: For I was an hungred, and ye gave Me meat: I was thirsty, and ye gave Me drink: I was a stranger, and ye took Me in: Naked, and ye clothed Me: I was sick, and ye visited Me: I was in prison, and ye came unto Me.
Then shall the righteous answer Him, saying, Lord, when saw we Thee an hungred, and fed Thee? Or thirsty, and gave Thee drink? When saw we Thee a stranger, and took Thee in? Or naked, and clothed Thee? Or when saw we Thee sick, or in prison, and came unto Thee?
And the King shall answer and say unto them, Verily I say unto you, Inasmuch as ye have done it unto one of the least of these My brethren, ye have done it unto Me.
Then shall He say also unto them on the left hand, Depart from Me, ye cursed, into everlasting fire, prepared for the devil and his angels: For I was an hungred, and ye gave Me no meat: I was thirsty, and ye gave Me no drink: I was a stranger, and ye took Me not

The Prophet's Life

in: naked, and ye clothed Me not: sick, and in prison, and ye visited Me not.
Then shall they also answer Him, saying, Lord, when saw we Thee an hungred, or athirst, or a stranger, or naked, or sick, or in prison, and did not minister unto Thee?
Then shall He answer them, saying, **Verily I say unto you, Inasmuch as ye did it not to one of the least of these, ye did it not to Me.** *And these shall go away into everlasting punishment: but the righteous into life eternal.* ~ Matthew 25:31-46

Interestingly, unlike any other prophet, the Lord often referred to Ezekiel as son of man, and Jesus also extensively used the same term to describe Himself during His earthly ministry.

Now back to Ezekiel, whom the Lord continued using to perform a diversity of prophetic acts, such as these:

And thou, son of man, take thee a sharp knife, take thee a barber's razor, and cause it to pass upon thine head and upon thy beard: then take thee balances to weigh, and divide the hair.
Thou shalt burn with fire a third part in the midst of the city, when the days of the siege are fulfilled: and thou shalt take a third part, and smite about it with a knife: and a third part thou shalt scatter in the wind; and I will draw out a sword after them.
Thou shalt also take thereof a few in number, and bind them in thy skirts.
Then take of them again, and cast them into the midst of the fire, and burn them in the fire; for thereof shall a fire come forth into all the house of Israel.
Thus saith the Lord God; This is Jerusalem: I have set it in the midst of the nations and countries that are round about her. And she hath changed My judgments into

The Prophet's Life

wickedness more than the nations, and My Statutes more than the countries that are round about her: for they have refused My judgments and My Statutes, they have not walked in them.

Therefore thus saith the Lord God; Because ye multiplied more than the nations that are round about you, and have not walked in My Statutes, neither have kept My judgments, neither have done according to the judgments of the nations that are round about you;

Therefore thus saith the Lord God; Behold, I, even I, AM against thee, and will execute judgments in the midst of thee in the sight of the nations.

And I will do in thee that which I have not done, and whereunto I will not do any more the like, because of all thine abominations.

Therefore the fathers shall eat the sons in the midst of thee, and the sons shall eat their fathers; and I will execute judgments in thee, and the whole remnant of thee will I scatter into all the winds.

Wherefore, as I live, saith the Lord God; Surely, because thou hast defiled My sanctuary with all thy detestable things, and with all thine abominations, therefore will I also diminish thee; neither shall Mine eye spare, neither will I have any pity. **A third part of thee shall die with the pestilence, and with famine shall they be consumed in the midst of thee: and a third part shall fall by the sword round about thee; and I will scatter a third part into all the winds, and I will draw out a sword after them.**

Thus shall Mine anger be accomplished, and I will cause My fury to rest upon them, and I will be comforted: and they shall know that I the Lord have spoken it in My zeal, when I have accomplished My fury in them.

Moreover I will make thee waste, and a reproach among the nations that are round about thee, in the sight of all that pass by.

So it shall be a reproach and a taunt, an instruction and an astonishment unto the nations that are round about

The Prophet's Life

thee, when I shall execute judgments in thee in anger and in fury and in furious rebukes. I the Lord have spoken it.
When I shall send upon them the evil arrows of famine, which shall be for their destruction, and which I will send to destroy you: and I will increase the famine upon you, and will break your staff of bread: So will I send upon you famine and evil beasts, and they shall bereave thee: and pestilence and blood shall pass through thee; and I will bring the sword upon thee. I the Lord have spoken it. ~ Ezekiel 5

It may have seemed disgraceful for Ezekiel to cut off the hair on his head and face, but it paled in comparison to the realities of the judgments his actions signified would come upon the land.

For good measure, prior to any verbal prophetic utterances, this is another of the times when the Lord used Ezekiel to perform prophetic acts as a sign to people:

The Word of the Lord also came unto me, saying, Son of man, thou dwellest in the midst of a rebellious house, which have eyes to see, and see not; they have ears to hear, and hear not: for they are a rebellious house.
Therefore, thou son of man, prepare thee stuff for removing, and remove by day in their sight; and thou shalt remove from thy place to another place in their sight: IT MAY BE THEY WILL CONSIDER, THOUGH THEY BE A REBELLIOUS HOUSE.
Then shalt thou bring forth thy stuff by day in their sight, as stuff for removing: and thou shalt go forth at even in their sight, as they that go forth into captivity.
Dig thou through the wall in their sight, and carry out thereby.
In their sight shalt thou bear it upon thy shoulders, and carry it forth in the twilight: thou shalt cover thy face, that thou see not the ground:

The Prophet's Life

FOR I HAVE SET THEE FOR A SIGN UNTO THE HOUSE OF ISRAEL.
And I did so as I was commanded: I brought forth my stuff by day, as stuff for captivity, and in the even I digged through the wall with mine hand; I brought it forth in the twilight, and I bare it upon my shoulder in their sight.
And in the morning came the Word of the Lord unto me, saying, Son of man, hath not the house of Israel, the rebellious house, said unto thee, What doest thou?
Say thou unto them, Thus saith the Lord God; This burden concerneth the prince in Jerusalem, and all the house of Israel that are among them.
Say, I AM YOUR SIGN: LIKE AS I HAVE DONE, SO SHALL IT BE DONE UNTO THEM: they shall remove and go into captivity.
And the prince that is among them shall bear upon his shoulder in the twilight, and shall go forth: they shall dig through the wall to carry out thereby: he shall cover his face, that he see not the ground with his eyes.
My net also will I spread upon him, and he shall be taken in My snare: and I will bring him to Babylon to the land of the Chaldeans; yet shall he not see it, though he shall die there. And I will scatter toward every wind all that are about him to help him, and all his bands; and I will draw out the sword after them. And they shall know that I AM the Lord, when I shall scatter them among the nations, and disperse them in the countries.
But I will leave a few men of them from the sword, from the famine, and from the pestilence; that they may declare all their abominations among the heathen whither they come; and they shall know that I AM the Lord.
Moreover the Word of the Lord came to me, saying, **Son of man, eat thy bread with quaking, and drink thy water with trembling and with carefulness;** And say unto the people of the land, Thus saith the Lord God of the inhabitants of Jerusalem, and of the

The Prophet's Life

land of Israel; They shall eat their bread with carefulness, and drink their water with astonishment, that her land may be desolate from all that is therein, because of the violence of all them that dwell therein. And the cities that are inhabited shall be laid waste, and the land shall be desolate; and ye shall know that I AM the Lord. ~ Ezekiel 12:1-20

Maybe now you can see how the Lord used Ezekiel as the primary source of inspiration for this book of prophetic fACTS and acts.

Some comics are referred to as "physical comedians" because they use the art of slapstick to generate laughter. During the time of silent films, men such as Charles Chaplin and Buster Keaton made people laugh based on their actions, to include their facial expressions. The inclusion of sound in film did not stop "The Three Stooges," Rowan Atkinson, Lucille Ball, Jackie Chan, and Jim Carrey from making people laugh with their actions. As I have stated in other books, such as **Roles & Responsibilities for Today's Prophets (of the Lord)**, prophets are more than speakers, they are communicators for the Lord. The Bible gives explanations of what the prophets' actions meant. Wise people should pay attention to what prophets do because it may foreshadow what the Lord is going to have them say. I am not sure what people thought Jesus was going to say and do when He saw people desecrating His Father's House. However, I know it was not a good sign when Jesus started making a scourge (John 2:13-22). Even though that was not a laughing matter, I know what comedian Bill Engvall would have said if he were there on that day with his current shtick. Bill would have recognized the sign.

Lastly, sometimes one of the most ominous signs from a prophet is when that messenger goes silent, which was what Jesus did for the most part prior to His crucifixion.

Chapter 4
Jeremiah

*Then Pashur smote Jeremiah the prophet,
and put him in the stocks that were in the high gate of
Benjamin, which was by the House of the Lord.*
~ Jeremiah 20:2

In addition to the previous chapter's citation about Jeremiah's marital status serving as a prophetic act, the Lord also had him perform these prophetic acts:

Thus saith the Lord unto me, Go and get thee a linen girdle, and put it upon thy loins, and put it not in water. So I got a girdle according to the Word of the Lord, and put it on my loins.
And the Word of the Lord came unto me the second time, saying, Take the girdle that thou hast got, which is upon thy loins, and arise, go to Euphrates, and hide it there in a hole of the rock.
So I went, and hid it by Euphrates, as the Lord commanded me.

The Prophet's Life

And it came to pass after many days, that the Lord said unto me, Arise, go to Euphrates, and take the girdle from thence, which I commanded thee to hide there.

Then I went to Euphrates, and digged, and took the girdle from the place where I had hid it: and, behold, the girdle was marred, it was profitable for nothing.

Then the Word of the Lord came unto me, saying, Thus saith the Lord, After this manner will I mar the pride of Judah, and the great pride of Jerusalem. This evil people, which refuse to hear My Words, which walk in the imagination of their heart, and walk after other gods, to serve them, and to worship them, shall even be as this girdle, which is good for nothing.

For as the girdle cleaveth to the loins of a man, so have I caused to cleave unto Me the whole house of Israel and the whole house of Judah, saith the Lord; that they might be unto Me for a people, and for a name, and for a praise, and for a glory: but they would not hear.

Therefore thou shalt speak unto them this Word; Thus saith the Lord God of Israel, Every bottle shall be filled with wine: and they shall say unto thee, Do we not certainly know that every bottle shall be filled with wine?

Then shalt thou say unto them, Thus saith the Lord, Behold, I will fill all the inhabitants of this land, even the kings that sit upon David's throne, and the priests, and the prophets, and all the inhabitants of Jerusalem, with drunkenness. And I will dash them one against another, even the fathers and the sons together, saith the Lord: I will not pity, nor spare, nor have mercy, but destroy them.

Hear ye, and give ear; be not proud: for the Lord hath spoken. Give glory to the Lord your God, before He cause darkness, and before your feet stumble upon the dark mountains, and, while ye look for light, He turn it into the shadow of death, and make it gross darkness.

But if ye will not hear it, My soul shall weep in secret places for your pride; and Mine eye shall weep sore, and

The Prophet's Life

run down with tears, because the Lord's flock is carried away captive.

Say unto the king and to the queen, Humble yourselves, sit down: for your principalities shall come down, even the crown of your glory. The cities of the south shall be shut up, and none shall open them: Judah shall be carried away captive all of it, it shall be wholly carried away captive. Lift up your eyes, and behold them that come from the north: where is the flock that was given thee, thy beautiful flock? What wilt thou say when He shall punish thee? For thou hast taught them to be captains, and as chief over thee: shall not sorrows take thee, as a woman in travail?

And if thou say in thine heart, Wherefore come these things upon me? For the greatness of thine iniquity are thy skirts discovered, and thy heels made bare.

Can the Ethiopian change his skin, or the leopard his spots? Then may ye also do good, that are accustomed to do evil.

Therefore will I scatter them as the stubble that passeth away by the wind of the wilderness. This is thy lot, the portion of thy measures from Me, saith the Lord; because thou hast forgotten Me, and trusted in falsehood.

Therefore will I discover thy skirts upon thy face, that thy shame may appear. I have seen thine adulteries, and thy neighings, the lewdness of thy whoredom, and thine abominations on the hills in the fields. Woe unto thee, O Jerusalem! Wilt thou not be made clean? When shall it once be? ~ Jeremiah 13

The Lord later used Agabus, a New Testament prophet, to perform a prophetic act while also using a girdle:

And the next day we that were of Paul's company departed, and came unto Caesarea: and we entered into the house of Philip the evangelist, which was one of the seven; and abode with him.

The Prophet's Life

And the same man had four daughters, virgins, which did prophesy.
And as we tarried there many days, there came down from Judaea a certain prophet, named Agabus.
And when he was come unto us, he took Paul's girdle, and bound his own hands and feet, and said, *Thus saith the Holy Ghost, So shall the Jews at Jerusalem bind the man that owneth this girdle, and shall deliver him into the hands of the Gentiles.*
And when we heard these things, both we, and they of that place, besought him not
Then Paul answered, What mean ye to weep and to break mine heart? For I am ready not to be bound only, but also to die at Jerusalem for the name of the Lord Jesus.
And when he would not be persuaded, we ceased, saying, ***The will of the Lord be done.*** ~ Acts 21:8-14

In another scenario, it was not the prophet who performed the prophetic act. God used a layperson's actions to give Jeremiah the Word of the Lord:

The Word which came to Jeremiah from the Lord, saying, Arise, and go down to the potter's house, and there I will cause thee to hear My Words.
Then I went down to the potter's house, and, behold, he wrought a work on the wheels. And the vessel that he made of clay was marred in the hand of the potter: so he made it again another vessel, as seemed good to the potter to make it.
Then the Word of the Lord came to me, saying, O house of Israel, cannot I do with you as this potter? saith the Lord. Behold, as the clay is in the potter's hand, so are ye in Mine hand, O house of Israel.
At what instant I shall speak concerning a nation, and concerning a kingdom, to pluck up, and to pull down, and to destroy it; If that nation, against whom I have

The Prophet's Life

pronounced, turn from their evil, I will repent of the evil that I thought to do unto them.
And at what instant I shall speak concerning a nation, and concerning a kingdom, to build and to plant it; If it do evil in My sight, that it obey not My voice, then I will repent of the good, wherewith I said I would benefit them.
Now therefore go to, speak to the men of Judah, and to the inhabitants of Jerusalem, saying, Thus saith the Lord; Behold, I frame evil against you, and devise a device against you: return ye now every one from his evil way, and make your ways and your doings good...
~ Jeremiah 18:1-11

Contrary to prophetic acts are false prophetic acts, for which the Lord gave Jeremiah this assignment:

In the beginning of the reign of Jehoiakim the son of Josiah king of Judah came this Word unto Jeremiah from the Lord, saying, **Thus saith the Lord to me; Make thee bonds and yokes, and put them upon thy neck,** *And send them to the king of Edom, and to the king of Moab, and to the king of the Ammonites, and to the king of Tyrus, and to the king of Zidon, by the hand of the messengers which come to Jerusalem unto Zedekiah king of Judah; And command them to say unto their masters, Thus saith the Lord of Hosts, the God of Israel; Thus shall ye say unto your masters; I have made the earth, the man and the beast that are upon the ground, by My great power and by My outstretched arm, and have given it unto whom it seemed meet unto Me.*
And now have I given all these lands into the hand of Nebuchadnezzar the king of Babylon, My servant; and the beasts of the field have I given him also to serve him. And all nations shall serve him, and his son, and his son's son, until the very time of his land come: and then many nations and great kings shall serve themselves of him.

The Prophet's Life

And it shall come to pass, that the nation and kingdom which will not serve the same Nebuchadnezzar the king of Babylon, **and that will not put their neck under the yoke of the king of Babylon***, that nation will I punish, saith the Lord, with the sword, and with the famine, and with the pestilence, until I have consumed them by his hand.*
Therefore hearken not ye to your prophets, nor to your diviners, nor to your dreamers, nor to your enchanters, nor to your sorcerers*, which speak unto you, saying, Ye shall not serve the king of Babylon: For they prophesy a lie unto you, to remove you far from your land; and that I should drive you out, and ye should perish.*
But the nations that bring their neck under the yoke of the king of Babylon, and serve him, those will I let remain still in their own land, saith the Lord; and they shall till it, and dwell therein. ~ Jeremiah 27:1-11

The Lord's will does not always lead down an easy path, but it always leads to Him, even if it means being chastised for a season.

Despite the Lord using the Prophet Jeremiah to give those clear instructions, to include warning about anyone who prophesies to the contrary, someone put the Word of the Lord to the test:

And it came to pass the same year, in the beginning of the reign of Zedekiah king of Judah, in the fourth year, and in the fifth month, that Hananiah the son of Azur the prophet, which was of Gibeon, spake unto me in the house of the Lord, in the presence of the priests and of all the people, saying, **Thus speaketh the Lord of hosts, the God of Israel, saying, I HAVE BROKEN THE YOKE OF THE KING OF BABYLON. Within two full years will I bring again into this place all the vessels of the Lord's house, that Nebuchadnezzar**

The Prophet's Life

king of Babylon took away from this place, and carried them to Babylon:
And I will bring again to this place Jeconiah the son of Jehoiakim king of Judah, with all the captives of Judah, that went into Babylon, saith the Lord: FOR I WILL BREAK THE YOKE OF THE KING OF BABYLON.

Then the Prophet Jeremiah said unto the Prophet Hananiah in the presence of the priests, and in the presence of all the people that stood in the House of the Lord, even the Prophet Jeremiah said, Amen: the Lord do so: the Lord perform thy words which thou hast prophesied, to bring again the vessels of the Lord's house, and all that is carried away captive, from Babylon into this place.

Nevertheless hear thou now this Word that I speak in thine ears, and in the ears of all the people; The prophets that have been before me and before thee of old prophesied both against many countries, and against great kingdoms, of war, and of evil, and of pestilence. The prophet which prophesieth of peace, **when the word of the prophet shall come to pass, then shall the prophet be known, that the Lord hath truly sent him.**

THEN HANANIAH THE PROPHET TOOK THE YOKE FROM OFF THE PROPHET JEREMIAH'S NECK, AND BRAKE IT.

And Hananiah spake in the presence of all the people, saying, Thus saith the Lord; Even so will I break the yoke of Nebuchadnezzar king of Babylon from the neck of all nations within the space of two full years.

And the prophet Jeremiah went his way.

Then the Word of the Lord came unto Jeremiah the prophet, **after that Hananiah the prophet had broken the yoke from off the neck of the Prophet Jeremiah,** saying, Go and tell Hananiah, saying, Thus saith the Lord; **Thou hast broken the yokes of wood;**

The Prophet's Life

but thou shalt make for them yokes of iron. *For thus saith the Lord of Hosts, the God of Israel; I have put a yoke of iron upon the neck of all these nations, that they may serve Nebuchadnezzar king of Babylon; and they shall serve him: and I have given him the beasts of the field also.* ~ Jeremiah 28:1-14

Hananiah's deception of the people, and his rebellion against God, resulted in the Lord using Jeremiah to prophesy judgment against him. Unfortunately for the unrepentant Hananiah, he died two months after Jeremiah's prophecy to him. Even though unwittingly on his part, Hananiah's death was a prophetic act to warn other prophets to not rebel against God, especially AFTER He tells them to repent. Also note what Christ Jesus said about Jezebel in Revelation 2:18-23.

There was a comparable situation to Hananiah's when King Ahab of Israel wanted King Jehoshaphat of Judah to join him in a battle against the Syrians to reclaim Ramoth Gilead. King Ahab had 400 prophets who sat at Queen Jezebel's table who said that God would give him the victory. But King Jehoshaphat had his doubts, so he wanted to inquire of a prophet of the Lord instead. Sadly, while they waited for Ahab's emissary to return with the Prophet Micaiah, the false prophets engaged in this false prophetic act:

And the king of Israel and Jehoshaphat the king of Judah sat each on his throne, having put on their robes, in a void place in the entrance of the gate of Samaria; and all the prophets prophesied before them.
And Zedekiah the son of Chenaanah made him horns of iron: and he said, THUS SAITH THE LORD, With these shalt thou push the Syrians, until thou have consumed them.
And all the prophets prophesied so, saying, Go up to Ramothgilead, and prosper: for the Lord shall deliver it into the king's hand. ~ 1 Kings 22:10-12

The Prophet's Life

Despite their prophetic actions, they were false prophets. The Lord was simply using them to lead King Ahab to his death. That was a part of God's judgment against the house of Ahab for his wickedness, and that of his wife Jezebel (1 Kings 21:17-29). Those prophets' actions are reflective of what is now written about the Antichrist and False Prophet:

Let no man deceive you by any means: for that day shall not come, except there come a falling away first, and that man of sin be revealed, the **son of perdition***; Who opposeth and exalteth himself above all that is called God, or that is worshipped; so that he as God sitteth in the Temple of God, shewing himself that he is God.*
Remember ye not, that, when I was yet with you, I told you these things?
And now ye know what withholdeth that he might be revealed in his time. For the mystery of iniquity doth already work: only he who now letteth will let, until he be taken out of the way.
And then shall that Wicked be revealed, whom the Lord shall consume with the Spirit of His mouth, and shall destroy with the brightness of His coming: **Even him, whose coming is after the working of satan with ALL POWER AND SIGNS AND LYING WONDERS, AND WITH ALL DECEIVABLENESS OF UNRIGHTEOUSNESS in them that perish;** *because they received not the love of the truth, that they might be saved. ~ 2 Thessalonians 2:3-10*

Regardless of how prophetic the acts may be or appear, what makes them truly prophetic is the entity behind them, whether it is God or satan. As Romans 8:31-39 proclaims, if God is for you, who can be against you?

Also, toward the end of Jeremiah's recorded ministry, some Judeans had asked him to inquire of the Lord on their behalf. Ten days later, the Word of the Lord came to Jeremiah with the Lord's will for the Judeans. But instead

The Prophet's Life

of obeying God, they accused Jeremiah of falsely prophesying and chose to seek refuge in Egypt as they had originally intended. They also took the remnant of Judah, to include Jeremiah and his servant Baruch to Egypt. In response, God had Jeremiah perform this prophetic act followed by the applicable Word of the Lord:

> *So they came into the land of Egypt:* **for they obeyed not the voice of the Lord:** *thus came they even to Tahpanhes.*
> *Then came the Word of the Lord unto Jeremiah in Tahpanhes, saying,* **Take great stones in thine hand, and hide them in the clay in the brickkiln, which is at the entry of Pharaoh's house in Tahpanhes, in the sight of the men of Judah;** *And say unto them, Thus saith the Lord of Hosts, the God of Israel; Behold, I will send and take Nebuchadrezzar the king of Babylon, My servant, and will set his throne upon these stones that I have hid; and he shall spread his royal pavilion over them. And when he cometh, he shall smite the land of Egypt, and deliver such as are for death to death; and such as are for captivity to captivity; and such as are for the sword to the sword. And I will kindle a fire in the houses of the gods of Egypt; and he shall burn them, and carry them away captives: and he shall array himself with the land of Egypt, as a shepherd putteth on his garment; and he shall go forth from thence in peace. He shall break also the images of Bethshemesh, that is in the land of Egypt; and the houses of the gods of the Egyptians shall he burn with fire.* ~ Jeremiah 43:7-13

Like Jonah, they found out that the Lord's Words and His will are inescapable, unless He truly grants people the freedom to choose.

Any seasoned prophet, especially one who has delivered messages to people who disobeyed God, chose their own way, and then suffered the consequences,

The Prophet's Life

knows it is best to choose God's will. Listening to and obeying the Lord has consequences, like the blessings and curses in Deuteronomy 28, which were predicated on the Israelites' obedience. Isaiah also prophesied this about the benefits of obeying the Lord:

> *If ye be **willing and obedient**, ye shall eat the good of the land: But if ye refuse and rebel, ye shall be devoured with the sword: for the mouth of the Lord hath spoken it.*
> ~ Isaiah 1:19-20

Any consequences that come with choosing God's will is better than those that stem from contradicting it. It is better if satan is against you than for God to be against you. God can protect you from satan, but satan cannot protect you from God. That is clear based on Revelation 19:20 when God executes His judgment against the Beast (Antichrist) and the False Prophet. It is also written:

> *For the Lord of Hosts hath purposed, and **who** shall disannul it? And His hand is stretched out, and **who** shall turn it back?* ~ Isaiah 14:27

Who?

Chapter 5
Jesus

I will raise them up a Prophet from among their brethren, like unto thee, and will put My Words in His mouth; and He shall speak unto them all that I shall command Him. And it shall come to pass, that whosoever will not hearken unto My Words which He shall speak in My name, I will require it of him.
~ Deuteronomy 18:18-19

Jesus fulfilled an astounding number of Messianic prophecies, each of which was a prophetic act to show that He was and is the Christ, the Son of God. When Jesus allowed His beloved friend Lazarus to die, it was for God's glory to show that He had power over death. When Jesus showed up four days postmortem, we see this exchange between Jesus and one of Lazarus's surviving sisters, Martha:

> *Jesus said unto her, I AM the Resurrection, and the Life: he that believeth in Me, though he were dead, yet shall he live: And whosoever liveth and believeth in Me shall never die. Believest thou this?*

The Prophet's Life

She saith unto Him, Yea, Lord: I believe that Thou art the Christ, the Son of God, which should come into the world. ~ John 11:25-27

But Jesus did a more significant prophetic act than to raise Lazarus from the dead to show His Messiahship. That is because Jesus was not the first to raise a person from the dead, Elijah and Elisha did that miracle (1 Kings 17:17-24, 2 Kings 4:11-37). Therefore, something that is often overlooked is the significance of Jesus opening the eyes of the blind, as was prophesied about Him (Isaiah 35:4-5, 42:7). The quintessential example of that is the man who was born blind, but Jesus gave him sight.

The Pharisees, with their hardened hearts, knew that a significant miracle had taken place, so they did their due diligence to verify it. Tragically, their actions were based on them being more interested in disproving the miracle so they could continue in their unbelief, and to cause others to believe that Jesus was NOT the Christ. But while interrogating the man who had been born blind, and his parents, the man said:

Now we know that God heareth not sinners: but if any man be a worshipper of God, **and doeth His will***, him He heareth.*
Since the world began was it not heard that ANY MAN OPENED THE EYES OF ONE THAT WAS BORN BLIND.
If this Man were not of God, He could do nothing.
~ John 9:31-33

The Pharisees despised the evidence of Jesus's Messiahship based on that incredibly significant prophetic act, so they cast the man away from them. What happened when he subsequently met Jesus is also very telling of the Lord's prophetic act to give sight to a man who was born blind:

The Prophet's Life

Jesus heard that they had cast him out; and when He had found him, He said unto him, Dost thou believe on the Son of God?
He answered and said, Who is He, Lord, that I might believe on Him?
And Jesus said unto him, Thou hast both seen Him, and it is He that talketh with thee.
And he said, Lord, I believe.
And he worshipped Him.
And Jesus said, **For judgment I AM come into this world, that they which see not might see; and that they which see might be made blind.**
And some of the Pharisees which were with Him heard these Words, and said unto Him, Are we blind also?
Jesus said unto them, If ye were blind, ye should have no sin: but now ye say, We see; **therefore your sin remaineth.** ~ John 9:35-41

The significance of Jesus giving that man sight cannot be overstated. For those who saw the evidence but opted to not believe Jesus, they were willfully blind to the Truth, and unless they repented, they would die in their sins.

Most of the Pharisees continued resisting Jesus by trying to ensnare Him and otherwise disprove that He was the Son of God. This is another of their counterproductive efforts to fight against Jesus:

Jesus went unto the mount of Olives.
And early in the morning He came again into the Temple, and all the people came unto Him; and He sat down, and taught them.
And the scribes and Pharisees brought unto Him a woman taken in adultery; and when they had set her in the midst, they say unto Him, Master, this woman was taken in adultery, in the very act.
Now Moses in the Law commanded us, that such should be stoned: but what sayest Thou?

The Prophet's Life

This they said, tempting Him, that they might have to accuse Him.
But Jesus stooped down, and with His finger wrote on the ground, as though He heard them not.
So when they continued asking Him, He lifted up Himself, and said unto them, He that is without sin among you, let him first cast a stone at her.
And again He stooped down, and wrote on the ground.
And they which heard it, being convicted by their own conscience, went out one by one, beginning at the eldest, even unto the last: and Jesus was left alone, and the woman standing in the midst.
When Jesus had lifted up Himself, and saw none but the woman, He said unto her, Woman, where are those thine accusers? Hath no man condemned thee?
She said, No man, Lord.
And Jesus said unto her, Neither do I condemn thee: go, and sin no more. ~ John 8:1-11

When the Pharisees violated the Law by trying to tempt Jesus (God), He initially ignored them (Deuteronomy 6:16). The Scripture does not state what Jesus wrote, but it is reminiscent of when King Belshazzar saw the hand of a man that wrote on the wall. When Daniel translated the handwriting, it was to let the king know that God had numbered his kingdom, he had been weighed and found wanting, and that his kingdom had been divided and given to others (Daniel 5). It is very possible, that like all of those in King Belshazzar's court who saw the writing but could not interpret it, that the Pharisees could not recognize Jesus's prophetic act and/or what His handwriting meant. And so, they kept trying to tempt Him (God) after He had ignored them. But even ignoring them was a prophetic act, a chance to reconsider their actions and repent before He got involved.

Also, even though she could have been put to death based on the allegations against her, the Lord forgave her (Leviticus 20:10). That forgiveness, along with every other

The Prophet's Life

time that Jesus forgave someone, were significant prophetic acts. That is evident based on what happened in Capernaum when four men brought a man with palsy to see Jesus for healing. But due to the crowd, they removed a section of the roof and lowered the man down on his bed to Jesus. These were the ensuing events:

> *When Jesus saw their faith, He said unto the sick of the palsy,* **Son, thy sins be forgiven thee.**
> *But there was certain of the scribes sitting there, and reasoning in their hearts, Why doth this Man thus speak blasphemies?* **WHO CAN FORGIVE SINS BUT GOD ONLY?**
> **And immediately when Jesus perceived in His Spirit that they so reasoned within themselves, He said unto them, Why reason ye these things in your hearts?** *Whether is it easier to say to the sick of the palsy, Thy sins be forgiven thee; or to say, Arise, and take up thy bed, and walk?* **But that ye may know that the Son of Man hath power on earth to forgive sins,** *(He saith to the sick of the palsy,) I say unto thee, Arise, and take up thy bed, and go thy way into thine house.*
> *And immediately he arose, took up the bed, and went forth before them all; insomuch that they were all amazed, and glorified God, saying, We never saw it on this fashion.* ~ Mark 2:5-12

As shown in how the testimony ends, prophetic acts are for God's glory. Throughout His earthly ministry, Jesus did things to glorify His Heavenly Father (Luke 2:48-49). Likewise, through the continued works of the Holy Spirit, He brings glory to Jesus (John 15:26-27, 16:13-14). Another noteworthy thing from above is how Jesus's prophetic act of forgiving the man's sins proved the Pharisees' point that Jesus was God. He forgave the man's sins and there was fruit of that forgiveness.

The Prophet's Life

Some other Pharisees also made the same mistake regarding how Jesus handled a sinful woman, whose sins He also forgave (Luke 7:36-50). There is also this account of a sinful woman who performed a prophetic act on Jesus, and as He said, we should honor her:

Now when Jesus was in Bethany, in the house of Simon the leper, there came unto Him a woman having an alabaster box of very precious ointment, and poured it on His head, as He sat at meat.
But when His disciples saw it, they had indignation, saying, To what purpose is this waste? For this ointment might have been sold for much, and given to the poor.
When Jesus understood it, He said unto them, Why trouble ye the woman? **For she hath wrought a good work upon Me.** *For ye have the poor always with you; but Me ye have not always.* **For in that she hath poured this ointment on My body, she did it for My burial.**
Verily I say unto you, Wheresoever this gospel shall be preached in the whole world, there shall also this, that this woman hath done, be told for a memorial of her.
~ Matthew 26:6-13

In addition to Jesus's authority over sickness was His authority over devils, some of whom caused diseases. It was a prophetic act whenever Jesus cast out a devil, a demonstration of His absolute authority over the kingdom of darkness. Jesus also delegated that authority to others to cast out devils in His name (Luke 10:1-20, Mark 16:15-18). To the condemnation of majority of the Pharisees, Sadducees, and scribes, even devils confessed that Jesus was the Christ when they would not:

And, behold, they cried out, saying, **What have we to do with Thee, Jesus, Thou Son of God?**
Art Thou come hither to torment us before the time?
~ Matthew 8:29

The Prophet's Life

Those devils even truthfully confessed what would happen to them in the end. They bowed their knees to Jesus just like how Dagon collapsed on his face (twice) when the Philistines placed the Ark of God next to him in his own temple (1 Samuel 5:1-5). Both events bear witness to the veracity of this:

Wherefore God also hath highly exalted Him, and given Him a name which is above every name: **That at the name of Jesus EVERY knee should bow,** *of things in heaven, and things in earth, and things under the earth;* **And that EVERY tongue should confess that Jesus Christ is Lord, to the glory of God the Father.**
~ Philippians 2:9-11

So, in addition to giving and/or restoring sight, casting out devils was another major sign of Jesus's Messiahship.

Behind each false god is a devil (Deuteronomy 32:16-17). That is why when the Lord sent Moses to Egypt, his prophetic acts were to glorify Yahweh by showing that He was more powerful than the gods/devils of Egypt. So even though the Egyptian sorcerers could replicate the first few signs/plagues, God always showed His superiority. When the sorcerers replicated the sign by turning their rods into serpents, Aaron's rod that had turned into a serpent swallowed theirs (Exodus 7:10-12). Similarly, when the sorcerers replicated the first two plagues, the pharaoh still had to rely on Moses and his God to end those plagues. But by the time the magicians did their incantations to replicate the third plague, the lice infestation, when they failed, they proclaimed to the pharaoh that it was the "Finger of God." From that point forward, pharaoh had no excuses for his continued rebellion against God (Exodus 8:18-19).

When Yahweh brought forth the tenth plague, please note that it was demonstrative of His explicit judgment of Egypt's gods:

The Prophet's Life

For I will pass through the land of Egypt this night, and will smite all the firstborn in the land of Egypt, both man and beast; **and against all the gods of Egypt I will execute judgment: I AM THE LORD.** ~ Exodus 12:29

The same thing applies to Jesus, and how this prophetic act showed His power and authority:

And the same day, when the even was come, He saith unto them, Let us pass over unto the other side.
And when they had sent away the multitude, they took Him even as He was in the ship.
And there were also with Him other little ships.
And there arose a great storm of wind, and the waves beat into the ship, so that it was now full.
And He was in the hinder part of the ship, asleep on a pillow: and they awake Him, and say unto Him, Master, carest Thou not that we perish?
And He arose, and rebuked the wind, and said unto the sea, Peace, be still.
And the wind ceased, and there was a great calm.
And He said unto them, Why are ye so fearful? How is it that ye have no faith?
And they feared exceedingly, and said one to another, **What manner of Man is this, that even the wind and the sea obey Him?** ~Mark 4:35-41

Jesus demonstrated His authority over His creations, the same way God had prepared a fish to swallow Jonah and then commanded it to spit him out (Jonah 1:17, 2:10). Likewise for commanding ravens to bring food to Elijah to sustain him during the drought (1 Kings 17:1-7). Also, we should not forget God's authority over the satan/devil, which shows that satan is the Lord's devil (Job 1-2).

Jesus instructed His disciples to perform this prophetic act, which shows that such actions are powerful, even when the affected individuals do not witness them:

The Prophet's Life

And into whatsoever city or town ye shall enter, enquire who in it is worthy; and there abide till ye go thence.
And when ye come into an house, salute it.
And if the house be worthy, let your peace come upon it: but if it be not worthy, let your peace return to you.
And whosoever shall not receive you, nor hear your words, when ye depart out of that house or city, shake off the dust of your feet.
Verily I say unto you, It shall be more tolerable for the land of Sodom and Gomorrha in the day of judgment, than for that city. ~ Matthew 10:11-15

Prior to Jesus's crucifixion, Pontius Pilate performed a prophetic act by washing his hands. It symbolized that he was not responsible for the shedding of the blood of Jesus, an innocent Man (Matthew 27:24). The apostles shaking the dust from their feet was indicative of the Lord being finished with a person or group, as was the case with King Saul. The king had rejected the Word of the Lord, so He eventually rejected Saul and "washed His hands" of him (1 Samuel 16:1).

Pontius Pilate was also involved in another prophetic act, one that took place after Jesus's crucifixion. The chief priests petitioned the governor to make changes to the inscription on Jesus's cross, which read (John 19:19):

Jesus Of Nazareth The King Of The Jews

But Pontius rebuffed their request by saying:

What I have written I have written. ~ John 19:22

Pilate's response was reflective of God's character, particularly His faithfulness to His Words. For example, the Lord told Jeremiah that He was watching over His Words to perform Them (Jeremiah 1:12). Yahweh also told Isaiah that His Words would not return unto Him

The Prophet's Life

void but would accomplish the purpose for which He sent Them.

I could communicate much more about Jesus's prophetic acts. In fact, this Book could have been entirely about His acts, but then it probably would have been called **The Prophetic fACTS of Jesus**.

I begin to close this chapter and book with some of Jesus's greatest prophetic acts, chronicles of the fulfillment of the purposes for which the Father sent Him to the earth. There was a misunderstanding based on what Jesus said and meant, but He foretold His greatest prophetic act when He said:

> *Destroy this Temple, and in three days I will raise it up.*
> *~ John 2:19*

People thought Jesus was referring to the Temple of God that King Solomon had originally built that was later destroyed and reconstructed. But Jesus was speaking about the Temple of His body. Jesus prophesied about His death, burial, and resurrection. Those things were prophetic acts to fulfill what Daniel had prophesied. The prophet foretold that the Messiah would come after Jerusalem (and the Temple of God) was rebuilt, and He would be killed before the city was destroyed again [which occurred in 70 A.D.]:

> *Know therefore and understand, that from the going forth of the commandment to **restore and to build Jerusalem unto the Messiah the Prince** shall be seven weeks, and threescore and two weeks: **the street shall be built again, and the wall, even in troublous times.***
> *And after threescore and two **weeks shall Messiah be cut off, but not for himself: and the people of the prince that shall come shall destroy the city and the sanctuary;** and the end thereof shall be with a*

The Prophet's Life

flood, and unto the end of the war desolations are determined. ~ Daniel 9:25-26

It can be said that Elisha performed a prophetic act after his death. It happened when, under duress, a deceased man's body was cast into the tomb where Elisha was buried. The man was resurrected when his lifeless body touched the deceased prophet's bones (2 Kings 13:20-21). That powerfully foreshadowed this epic event at the time of Jesus's death:

Jesus, when He had cried again with a loud voice, yielded up the Ghost.
And, behold, the veil of the temple was rent in twain from the top to the bottom; and the earth did quake, and the rocks rent; **And the graves were opened; AND MANY BODIES OF THE SAINTS WHICH SLEPT AROSE, and came out of the graves after His resurrection, and went into the holy city, and appeared unto many.**
Now when the centurion, and they that were with him, watching Jesus, saw the earthquake, and those things that were done, they feared greatly, saying, **Truly this was the Son of God.** ~ Matthew 27:50-54

Those events even caused a Roman centurion to acknowledge that Jesus was the Son of God. But there was more, the icing on the cake. Jesus performed a prophetic act through His resurrection from the dead that shows that death has no power over Him, or His children. And, as Jesus later told John:

I AM He that liveth, and was dead; and, behold, I AM alive for evermore, Amen; and have the keys of hell and of death. ~ Revelation 1:18

God outsmarted satan yet again and redeemed mankind.

The Prophet's Life

Time for another "Praise Break!!!"

The devil seemingly missed all the signs that he was doomed, for it is written:

> *Which none of the princes of this world knew: for had they known it,* ***THEY WOULD NOT have crucified the Lord of Glory.*** *But as it is written, Eye hath not seen, nor ear heard, neither have entered into the heart of man, the things which God hath prepared for them that love Him.* ~ 1 Corinthians 2:8-9

Now the Lord Jesus Christ can say to the devil: **"Checkmate!"**

EPILOGUE

When Elijah obeyed the Word of the Lord to make Elisha the prophet over Israel in his stead, he simply removed his mantle and draped it over Elisha. Yet, with that prophetic act, and no words from the prophet, Elisha knew what it meant. As a result, he killed the pair of oxen he had been plowing behind and cooked their meat with the yoke he had used to join and maneuver them. Then Elisha requested to bid his parents farewell before following Elijah to one day assume his position as the prophet over Israel. Interestingly, despite Elisha's recognition of Elijah's prophetic act, and responding appropriately to it, Elijah said:

Go back again: for what have I done to thee?
~ 1 Kings 19:20

Elisha's response after Elijah placed his mantle upon him foreshadowed how Jesus would approach some of His future disciples, the apostles. And, by simply saying, "Follow Me," they would drop what they were doing to follow a Man, Who, at the time, they were not even sure was the Christ. Hence, when Jesus performed a prophetic act by calming the sea, His disciples marvelled and said:

What manner of Man *is this, that even the winds and the sea obey Him!* ~ Matthew 8:27

Elijah's God-given authority over nature foreshadowed Jesus. Even the prophet's mantle was linked to the Christ. Elijah used his mantle to cover Elisha as a sign of his prophetic calling. Elisha served Elijah for years and saw when Elijah used his mantle to part the River Jordan (2 Kings 2). That was the day when the Lord was going to take Elijah into heaven. Elisha knew this so he asked

The Prophet's Life

Elijah for a double portion of his Spirit (anointing). Elijah said it would be granted IF Elisha saw him being taken into heaven, which he did. Shortly after, when the chariot and the horses of fire swept Elijah from the earth, his mantle fell on the ground. Elisha picked up the mantle and started his ministry as the senior prophet over Israel, and therefore the world. The first miracle Elisha did was to repeat what Elijah had done by using that mantle to part the River Jordan again so he could cross back to the other side. Those events point to how Jesus's disciples would witness His ascension back into heaven. Jesus had said those who believe Him would do greater works than Him because He was returning to the Father (John 14:12). Interestingly, Elisha has more recorded miracles in the Bible than Elijah. In addition, upon his ascension, Elijah's mantle fell on the earth, which served as a sign of Elisha's empowerment from God. Likewise, after Jesus's ascension to heaven, the same Holy Spirit He had, descended on the earth like a rushing mighty wind to empower His disciples (Acts 2:2).

Sometimes people overlook the things of God because they wanted and/or expected to hear His voice so they miss what He communicated. Prophets are the Lord's communications devices, which means they sometimes communicate what the Lord is revealing via prophetic acts. Those acts typically, but may not always, come with the applicable Word of the Lord. We must be in tune with what the Spirit of the Lord is communicating, in the same way how Jesus simply looked at Peter and he knew he was in trouble (Luke 22:59-62).

Our relationship with the Lord, as with our relationships with humans, is not limited to what is said, it is also about what is communicated. As this book has shown, one of the ways the Lord communicated in the past, and therefore still communicates today, is by using prophetic acts. That was the case the last time I saw my paternal grandmother and she gave me that look.

The Prophet's Life

ABOUT THE AUTHOR

Kollin L. Taylor is a Jamaican born American combat veteran of battles in the natural and spiritual realms. The Lord Jesus Christ called him to "Minister to the people." He fulfills that mandate in a multitude of ways, such as through the following published books:

Exposed Part 1: The Prelude
Exposed Part 2: Romantic Relationships
Exposed Part 3: Vida
Exposed Part 4: The Journey Continues
Metamorphosis: The New Me
The Phenom: From My Soul
The Aftermath: When the Smoke Clears and the Dust Settles
Resilience: Bend, Don't Break
Perspective: A New Point of View
The Anatomy of a Heartbreak: When SAMson Met Delilah
Round 2: The Battle Continues
Round 3: Still Fighting
Cool Breeze: Irie Man!
Finding Joy in YOU: The Gift of Eternal Life
The Path to Enlightenment
Minister to the People: Answering His Calling
Australia: A Journey Down Under
Wrongfully Accused: When Innocence Is Not Enough
The Sidelines: Those Who Can...
Flirting with Disaster
The Sound of a Fallen Tree
Survival
Humble Pie: A Gift from God
Second Chance: Worthy of Redemption
God's Kitchen: His Slow-Cooked Stew
God, the Love of my Life
God Speaks to My Soul

The Prophet's Life

On Trial: A Test of My Faith
Closet Christian: If You Deny Him, He Will Deny You
Soul Food: Thanks Lord, for My Daily Bread
Knowledge is Power: Before You Do What You're Told, Know What You're Being Told
Labor Pains... Waiting to Push!
Breakthrough: When Jesus Sets You Free
Born Again: Renew Your Mind with the Holy Spirit
Holy Spirit Led: My Steps are Ordered
Raised in the Wilderness: Rogue Reformers, Rallying the Remnant
So, You Want to be a Prophet... ARE YOU CRAZY?
The Process: The Refiner's Fire
So, You Want to Marry a Prophet... ARE YOU CRAZY?
The Prophet and the witch: Under the Influence
The Devil's War Against Your God-Ordained Marriage
The Blind Seer: Seeing in the Dark
Psalmists Arise: Beyond the Music
Intercessory Birth Pangs: The Prophetic Intercessor
The Watchman: What Do You See?
Apostolic Authority: Unleashing Heaven on Hell
Child Soldier: Train Up a Child for [Spiritual] Warfare
RelationWITCH: Godly Wait or the devil's Bait
Apostle in Training: Suffering Shame for Jesus's Name
It May Be DEMONic AND You Need Deliverance IF...The Life of a Tormented Christian
Roles & Responsibilities for Today's Prophets (of the Lord)
FOUR Shades of Prophets: The Slippery Slope to Hell
The Prophet's Life: Prophetic fACTS, Prophetic Acts

The Prophet's Life

Author Photo
by
Mikiel